Memories, Musings and Moments . . .

PHYLLIS GRIGGS

authorHOUSE®

AuthorHouse™
1663 Liberty Drive, Suite 200
Bloomington, IN 47403
www.authorhouse.com
Phone: 1-800-839-8640

This book is a work of non-fiction. Unless otherwise noted, the author and the publisher make no explicit guarantees as to the accuracy of the information contained in this book and in some cases, names of people and places have been altered to protect their privacy.

© 2007 Phyllis Griggs. All rights reserved.

No part of this book may be reproduced, stored in a retrieval system, or transmitted by any means without the written permission of the author.

First published by AuthorHouse 12/3/2007
ISBN: 978-1-4343-3915-7 (sc)
ISBN: 978-1-4343-3914-0 (hc)

Printed in the United States of America
Bloomington, Indiana

This book is printed on acid-free paper.

Contents

Musings

Morning Thoughts 3
Aging Dreams 5
Christmas Joy 7
The Grocery Store 9
Excitement– Island Style 13
Laser Eyes 15
The Park That Wasn't 17
The Water Grasshopper 19
Tears 21
God Bless America 23
Kaleidoscope Evening 27
Play Ball! 29
Heroes 31
Success Story 33

Family

The Child Brigade 37
A Miserable Merry Christmas 39
I Remember Roy 43
My Grandmother's Robe 45
Dad Said It Was Easy 49

Valentine Mom 51
Family Affairs 53
Uncle Bud 55
Antiquity 57
The Moms 59
Christmas in Virginia 61
The Forever Mom 63

Journeys
Ireland– The Journey 67
Land Of Contrast 69
Egypt– The Journey 73

Old Friends
The Last of the Real Cowboys 79
Best Friends 81
Robin Hood 83
The Littlest Rancher 85
The Perfect Shell 89
New Year's Cowlamity 91

Events
The President Present 95
The Chiefs And Me 99
The Day the Planes Came 103

Valley Friends
I Miss My Friend 109
The Ferryboat Ride 111
The Simpson Place 113

All The Things You Are 115

The Guys My Age 117

Weird Stuff 121

The Christmas Babies 123

Jacque's Mom 125

Just Passing Through 127

The Donut Shop Lovers 129

Dad And Me 131

Letter to Larry 135

Monica's Angels 137

The Barbecue Guys 139

River Song 143

My Chief 145

Animal Love

Puppy love 149

The City Slicker 153

Little Dog Lost 155

Good Girl 157

Rocky 161

For *Pity's* Sake 163

Bess Brown 167

Bird Watch 169

They're Baaaack!! 171

The Hawk & I 175

Wings Of The Wind 177

For The Birds 179

The Nutria 183

Bob 185

Prologue

While, over the past years, I have contemplated writing the proverbial "book" I never really got in the mindset of the author. I have put to paper, over these past years many, many articles, letters and thoughts. Nothing so important as to cause a reader to clutch his/her heart and immediately send it off to Oprah, but thoughts that I believe we all have– friends we all have and relatives, good, bad and ugly out there and pets that we love and care for over the years.

These are just those thoughts. Many from a Rapid City, South Dakota farm girl, who twirled through the snowy night to pull a calf or who knew real cowboys who roped and rode in those Black Hills of South Dakota.

Moving to McAllen in 1970 changed my World from saddles and secretarial work to Donuts, Laundry and a fourteen year stint as a City Commissioner and Mayor Pro-Tem.

To tell you about McAllen would take another book, but I will tell you that this Rio Grande Valley, now my home, will take you and nourish you and love you as its own. I am grateful for McAllen and the people, who live, work and provide here. These people I have loved and cared about, who have cared about me, too many to mention, but not too many to think of as I write this prologue.

Read through this jumble of articles, many sad and many funny, but my thoughts and ideas over these past 15 years. I hope you enjoy them and recognize an old friend or two.

I want to dedicate this book to the three people who have changed my life over its course.

Ep Howe– My inspiration
Mac Chambers– My optimism
Tracy Griggs– My daughter, my best friend

Musings

I pour over these articles and I wonder if "musings" is the correct terminology?

Spending my early mornings on the diving board observing the back pasture and the creatures therein. My mind wanders to the other great questions of life; can the grocery store be THAT difficult, am I really that old and is the premise of a "park that wasn't there" actually called "musing"?

You will have to determine these (and other pertinent) questions as you peruse this chapter of thoughts and memories. Through the mind of the not-so-gifted, and into a mind filled with childlike wonder— too young for senility, too old for childish behavior.

Morning Thoughts

Early of the morning, when others are plumping up their pillows to turn to get another hour sleep, I prowl through the back yard leafing through my catalog of memories. The animals are quiet in the barn, but the rooster meets the challenge of the neighboring rooster's crow, and he crows stridently out there in the dark.

The air is cool and the stars remain in the sky, and occasionally, this particular morning, I see a flash of heat lightning streaking across the horizon. On the diving board, I look, as usual, toward the old Simpson place, wishing for the hundredth time that I could see their light on in the kitchen as Billy poured himself that early morning cup of coffee. But it is quiet over there, the "park" waiting for the children to come and play mid-day.

The duck houses are empty now, babies gone off to water with moms and I ponder on the hows and whys of their lifestyles. The babies are born in the duck houses, high off the ground, and almost as soon as they are hatched, they climb from the house, up the little metal webbing and jump to the ground and are hastened away by their moms. We saw them once, mother leading and babies hopping along behind, wending their way across the pasture to some distant swimming hole, I guess.

I have the CD playing softly and I sing along catching the words sometimes a bit too slowly, and sometimes, gratifyingly, right on the money. My big dog, Bob, sits where I sit (unlike his predecessor, Slick, who investigated each and every nook and cranny of the yard every morning) and we, each in our own fashion, I imagine, wonder what awaits us on this day.

By 6:30 AM I am ready to return to my "real" life there in the house, to do the things are there to do: bed making, clothes putting away– and the challenge of picking up all of Bob's toys from the bedroom floor (and MY shoes from every room in the house). Then off to work.

Mornings have always been mine. Back in South Dakota, I would go and sit on the bales of hay that were stacked outside the corral. I dreamed dreams of traveling and gray horses and a very small pinky ring. My wants were never great big, and who would have dreamed so big as to live in the Rio Grande Valley, to stand upon a diving board and see the World?

Life is good in McAllen, Texas.

Aging Dreams

When I was younger I dreamed I could fly; soaring above the ground, gently dipping down but for the briefest of moments and then to soar to the skies again. It was always pretty much the same, the way it would start, that is. I would be standing, talking with someone, and I would suddenly have that "urge" - I would take a deep breath and, to their utter amazement, and to mine, I would leave the ground, foot by foot, until I could swoop and soar and see the green pastures below. It was a joyous event, this flying business, and I remember laughing aloud as I passed overhead.

I dreamed of elevators, also... Elevators going up and down and sideways, as well. Elevators swinging precariously in the elevator shaft, with me waiting at the door - trying to jump in; and once inside, to cling to the sides as we careened through building after building. One particular elevator came back again and again. An elevator that had black wrought iron bars in front of it, and inside? Inside was red velvet wallpaper. While I felt no particular fear of this elevator, I saw it in intricate detail. A small stool in the front, to my right as I got in, a crank, I assume, to make it go up and down. There were two sets of doors on the front, the wrought iron door that smoothly opened OUT, much like a house door, and a door inside that slid shut when you boarded.

Elevators really aren't that big of a deal, unless, of course, like me there in Rapid City, South Dakota, you had never ridden in an elevator. But, there, in Rapid City, South Dakota, I dreamed of elevators. I dreamed of elevators even after I had ridden in elevators, no change. They still swung precariously in oversized elevator shafts and I still dreamed of the wrought iron elevator with the red velvet interior.

As I have aged, going from believing that, someday, someone would ask me to take their fabulous gray Quarter Horse mare, as a gift, to knowing that if I wanted a gray Quarter Horse mare, I have to find her and BUY her. I no longer believe that I can place all of the puppies that are sold in roadside stands into homes that love them and take care of them. Reality comes with age, they say, but for some reason, with me, age came alone...

I have been worried that growing old means growing UP. I can attest that this is simply not true. Just because I now know that I am never going to receive that gift horse, that great gray mare, and just because I know in my heart, that those puppies won't all go to good homes, it doesn't keep me from believing that there is a magic in our lives, miracles that transcend all of the realities.

Miracles, magic, the things that happen to you as you grow older -I took a ride in the wrought iron elevator of my dreams when I was 40 - it was in Monte Carlo, Monaco - honest! Red velvet wall paper and little stool, - just as I dreamed. I bought my own gray mare when I was 50 and I watch her from my bedroom window. She's almost everything I dreamed she'd be, even though she's as spoiled and willful as she is beautiful. (My dream didn't demand her to be 100% perfect - ok?)

Walking on the beach last year, feeling depressed and lonely, and a wave splashed ashore, bearing with it a crucifix fish - I had never seen one before, but then, I guess I had never needed one before. It was new magic for me. It opened my eyes and my head to fresh miracles and new magic.

However, here on the eve of my 60th birthday, I wish only for old miracles - just let me fly in my dreams again - for the rest of my life.

Christmas Joy

Christmas just around the corner - again? I can hardly believe that it was a whole year ago that all of those conflicting Christmas time blues circled my Casa. The joy over the season, but.... I find that I am a bit (?) hyper active over, well, just about everything!

The gifts that I promised myself I would not get for my daughter have already arrived at her home. She is probably wearing and/or using them as I write. Guilt, of course, over my baby NOT having anything to open on Christmas morning, will drive me to another reign of shopping terror at the Mall and another batch of goodies will be sent out before the 25th.

The great designer tie I bought for Rodd no longer looks as good as it did when I bought it, and I guess I'll just put it up there with the purse that I bought for Sylvia last year that I didn't like after I got home. The "gourmet" coffee that looked so expensive and tasteful at Sam's now sits, waiting to be wrapped and it rather looks like the bargain that it was - darn! It was for my ex-husband's wife - oh well, she'll just have to live with it..

Sure, buying gifts is great fun - but then there is the WRAPPING. You sometimes cut the paper two inches too small for the gift - it's the last piece in that particular design so you have to cover one end with the battered remainder of the roll. (Or sometimes, after a particularly arduous wrapping fiasco, you just leave the end of the box exposed, thinking that no one will notice anyway!!) There is the added pressure of sometimes have TOO much paper. Being faced with cutting off the end - AFTER the rest of the box is wrapped - or artfully wadding up the end and taping it down (a particular favorite of mine) is not pleasant.

This is a worrisome season as well. I am troubled thinking of the people for whom I would not dream of getting a present getting me a present. Should I get them something "just in case" and make certain that I like it really well "just in case" they DON'T get me something so I can keep it?

Is a person duty bound to respond to Christmas "form letters" telling how every member of the family received a promotion or straight A's? Or, if personal problems are revealed, should they be addressed in YOUR return card? "Too bad about your sister's divorce - I had no idea that her husband had a substance abuse problem and would use her for batting practice.. But, thanks for telling me (and the rest of your acquaintances) about it." - Merry Christmas!!

Aside from those pressing worries, what a wonderful time of year!! We get to wear bells and Santa hats and mistletoe and go to parties and do nice things for people that we really like. We get to be openly thankful for our lives and we can be as children once again and look to the skies for the miracles that we KNOW can happen this time of year.

It's also the only time of year when I can sing at the top of my lungs and know full well that I know ALL the words to almost ALL of the songs! JOY TO THE WORLD! I love this time of year - God bless us every one.

The Grocery Store

Grocery shopping is a chore for me; and getting me to the Grocery Store about takes that "act of Congress" we always hear about! But, life is about duty and grocery shopping, in my mind, is my duty– so, once a month whether I need to go or not, I go.

Before the actual event takes place, I stand somberly in front of the refrigerator– perusing the contents. Nothing! In some homes, I feel certain that "nothing" means bit and pieces of stuff– bacon and fruit and cheese and luncheon meats. At my house, in my refrigerator, when I say "nothing"– I mean "nothing". Large shiny glass shelves, may, perhaps contain a tub of margarine and jars of mayonnaise, ketchup, various jellies– and nothing. The mystery drawers– below– have plastic bags of things– some too far gone to recognize– an old ear of corn for Cowboy, oranges and a tomato on the far edge of old age– wrinkled, not dead, but too late for life support.

And, I know, it's *time*.

The *Grocery Store* could probably intimidate me were I not careful– I remember the first time I had to go to the "new" store– they gave us maps to find our way around. (I always wish I had saved my copy.) I vividly remember the first time in that new store– I walked in filled with anticipation, and walked out carrying a package of toilet paper that filled rear of my 4-Runner. The small packages must have been cleverly hidden away, and, in a panic, I opted to take what I found and go with it! That was the trip that they told me that "No wonder you can't find the bread, of course, it's not in the bakery!" Ahhhh.

So, anyhow, Saturday afternoon, when real people who have real lives are home doing whatever it is that real people do who have real lives; I was glumly pushing the grocery cart through the wide aisles of <u>my</u> grocery store. (A grocery store becomes "yours" when it is closer than your old store!) Now I will be the first to admit that I cheer up considerably when I am actually *in* the store. (Especially if I'm hungry!) Wow– does that what-ever-it-is ever look good– I'll just get two of 'em... The golden brown chicken that has been rotisseried somewhere in the store beckons to me– and, please, God, don't let me pass by when they bring those hot loaves of bread out of the oven!

Of course, in the midst of the shopping gluttony, you <u>have</u> to run into several friends (they are just coming from or going to someplace fancy. They look really swell and dressed up; I have on my slaps and Montalvo T-shirt hanging over a pair of shorts that once were white.) Actually, I haven't figured out if I feel more uncomfortable at how I look or that THEY feel more uncomfortable at how I look. Oh well.

Ok, then– on to the shopping, past the meat counter and on to the– hey! Get a load of that sign!! "Chicken thighs– 59 cents a pound!!" Those chicken thighs had enormous appeal to me today– I almost shouted out "Can you believe this? 59 cents a pound!!" To understand the significance of this, is that chicken thighs are what Slick eats– so to see packages of 10 chicken thighs for some $2.50 is very exciting! You're a cheap date tonight, Slickers!

Waiting in the check-out line, my eye, quite naturally, strays to The National Enquirer– "Big Foot Captured in the Wild– Has the World's oldest Social Security number"– have you ever noticed– there is no way you can finish an article before they check you out? So, with joking whispers, you tell the clerk "I really never take these home, but I have started on this . . . . ." Yeh, yeh.

Usually, while loitering there with basket filled with non-essentials, I remember the critical items that I have forgotten– one person in front of me and two behind– do I have the time? Can I make it? Should I take cart out of line and go "back in" - ? Nahh– I'll save it for next month– Who needs dish soap anyhow? How important can bread be? 'sides that, I have a National Enquirer to read..

Excitement- Island Style

It's just a little Island house but it sits down the road from the statuesque towers that house the *"games"*. For want of a better word, I must call the diving, and plunging and leaping, the *"games"* and on a weekend, I sit on the deck of my stick house and watch and listen to the people who do all of the things over there that I could never do. I have pondered upon this "never" thing, and am certain that I could and would never leap from extreme heights much less jump from those tall towers. While I watch, the elevator goes up, up, up and a lone diver comes down, down, down, I shiver sitting there watching. BUNGI!!

One of the other towers holds the giant swing where two people can sit and then they are shot into the air– like on huge rubber bands– reaching almost to the tops of the tower. I can tell who is doing what as I hear the boys "whoop" and the girls scream– all in fun and excitement. They spring up and down, whooping and screaming and enjoying the excitement of the evening.

The third "game" is like a giant slingshot– two to three people are securely fastened into the harness– lying down– facing forward– then they are hoisted up to the tallest tower by means of a pulley and other cables. When they are to the top of the pulley tower, they are released and they fly into the Padre Island air– straight down, and then miraculously back into the air.

One evening, Bob (my big dog) and I wandered down to inspect the games— there was a line of young people waiting to board one or the other of them. The attendants were efficient and bolstered the courage of the timid soul who couldn't make up his or her mind. I wasn't convinced that an old girl such as me should ever get aboard, and I moseyed back to my little house to watch and wonder.

Back in South Dakota, a million years ago, we did the dangerous things too, I guess— we drove on Sheridan Lake's icy surface— throwing snow balls and careening just out of reach of the other cars. We floated in inner tubes across that same Lake when summer came, and I never realized that I couldn't float on my own, much less swim. We thought we lived life on the edge, and, perhaps we did. We just didn't have to reach high into the night skies to get our thrills. Is it all the same, I wonder? As teenagers, do we, in fact, have to face all of those things before we can successfully "grow up"?

Now, as an adult, I find my excitement in a myriad of ways, the baby Blue Martins are moving around, and my goat, Dinah had a baby. I sit in the back yard and I am excited by the prospect of new flowers on my Desert Willow and await the brilliant red buds that will come on my Kapok tree.

You have to take your excitement where you find it, I guess.

Laser Eyes

The more I thought about it, the better the idea seemed. It told me, right there on the radio (and ya gotta believe what you hear on the radio, right?) that there was nothing to it, just come in for a "free analysis" and within days, perfect vision (or near to it) would be mine.

After several aborted tries– calling the number listed in the advertisement and missing one number and getting the "bzz-bzz" sound, calling after hours to be told by a pleasant voice to call during "Office" hours, and finally, finally connecting with someone incredibly nice who set up the appointment. The appointment was for the following week, and during the next few days, I had several misgivings. The fact that I hadn't spoken with my own eye doctor, and the fact that he could be quite cranky when he was cut from the loop was a major consideration.

Sitting there in the *big* chair, the glass mechanicals in front of me, the board with large letters (and larger letters) at the end of the room, I broached the subject. "Hey Biek, I want to go and get the laser surgery on my eyes!" He gave me the across the top of his glasses look. Ut oh! I blundered on "You know, I am so sick of my glasses riding down on my nose (look here– see the dents on the sides?) I can't lie on the sofa and watch TV any more because I can't see it without my glasses and when I wear my glasses, they get all pushy and crooked and I - -" Another across the top of his glasses look– he began the "your eyes aren't all that bad, you aren't having any problems and–" Then the look of resignation, "You're doing it already, aren't you?" - Yup, tomorrow.

The next morning, sitting in the waiting room inside the waiting rooms, clad in blue booties over my shoes, and a bowl cover on the head, I was ready for the procedure. My pal, Jacque Gillespie sat along side me; purse clutched in her little hands (ever notice when a woman is nervous she clutches her purse?) and across the room sat a man– blue booties in place and bowl cover on head. We eyed each other suspiciously– "You nervous?" I asked. He said "nah"– "well, maybe a little.." They took me first and I cast an "ut oh" glance back at him

The room was cool and comfortable, and the attendants were all attired much like me– including face masks however. I felt like I was in a roomful of robbers there for a moment, but still wasn't nervous. Lie back now, stretch out– stare up at tiny red dot.

Ten pain free minutes later, I am walking down the hallway, eye covers attached to my face by virtue of scotch tape– seeing clear as a bell. Hey, Doc– does this mean my glasses may be donated to the Lions Club? You bet, and there is the box right in front of me. (I cast a quick look into the waiting man in the waiting room– grimace, just for him and stroll on down the hallway (ya gotta get your kicks when you can!).

Three days later I am reading my book, watching my TV, and using my computer– glasses free. Not exactly "free" I must say, but reasonable. Good decision, Griggs!

The Park That Wasn't

It was almost a year ago now that I stood on my diving board, looking toward the Simpson property. The property was vacant then– just the fireplace standing, and the birds searching for houses that weren't there. While I was troubled in losing my friends and neighbors, I rationalized that there would be a park there, a park that would, eventually have boxes for the birds and walking trails and things that would make others love the property as the Simpson's did.

Today, as I stand on that same diving board, I see slides and swings and children's outside toys at the old Simpson property, and I reminisce about the poem from Robert L. Stevenson about "how I love to go up in the swing, up in the air so high". I now feel secure that the birds most likely will not go back there, but will come to my place to be safe from playing children and know the peace that only an undeveloped area can give them.

The fence that surrounds the Simpson Park is chain link, and my Guineas occasionally fly the journey of the brave– over the fence. To be rescued by me late of an evening (when they forgot how they got there) and it is quiet in the Simpson Park for the most part.

Across the front of the Simpson Park, there is also a chain link fence, with a sign that reads "No Trespassing– Violators will be subject to a $500 fine– City Of McAllen." The children who play within, laughing from swing sets and teeter-totters and slides are the only children who play there. They are the children from the adjacent subdivision– where there is no fence– and they are welcome.

Strange to think of a park within a City that is not for all City children. A park owned by a City that keeps the front gate secured and the side gates open. I puzzle over these strange sets of events, and I wonder "is this the park that wasn't there?"

If that is the case, could the Simpson's come back and just let the neighbor children play in their back yard? Could the purple martin houses go back up and the duck houses full again? Could their dogs romp in the front yard, and could Billy barbecue on the patio again? Could we, once again, call across the fence and hand dishes of freshly made stew through the gate?

I know their new telephone number!

The Water Grasshopper

Who was it that fooled the summer away while the ants made ready for winter? I believe, if I recall my parables, it was the grasshopper. I kinda feel like that myself– I look around my yard at my water intensive plants and trees– and, of course, that blasted Koi pond that runs dry on a weekly basis and wonder what *was* I thinking? I have lived in a world that always, I mean ALWAYS had water. There was no problem other than the occasional big water bill when the horse trough ran over (unnoticed) and I had to splash in through the stalls to rectify the problem. But other than that, at the turn of a tap, at the click of a sprinkler, clear, sparkling water ran forth with reckless abandon.

I have literally frittered water away during the summers of my life, and now the winters of no water are upon us. It's not Chicken Little looking to the sky and feeling certain that the sky is falling. The sky IS falling, water wise, and while hindsight is a tremendous motivator, it does nothing to save the dying trees in my yard beyond the watering line. The sad realization that water is *now* (and wasn't it always?) precious and I mourn the poor judgment that prompted me to continue to add new trees to my yard, and ponds that evaporate our water in the steaming summer sun.

You see, I really want to do what is right. I want to save the water and to conserve and to be a good citizen. I really want my water usage to drop the 20% the City is requesting, but my heart is aching for my trees, my plants, and the living things that will no longer be living without water. Sneaking water isn't an option; for soon, there will be no water to sneak. My mind has been economizing on water; I have been contemplating running my washer water out into my back yard onto my more precious of plants. Where does the shower water go? What else can I do to keep the living living?

The water dilemma is not a today problem, not a "when winter comes it'll be ok" problem; it is a problem with monumental consequences. It's just not going away. I am just trying to make peace with it— I find that I am making deals with myself— ok, I'll only water the lawn once a week, but I will individually water <u>only</u> the plants and trees one a week. Does THIS help?

The animals suffer now, between the lack of water and the heat and I try to keep mindful of this and sit a dish of water outside of the office for the birds and those homeless cats we see pass. The grass in my pasture is parched and Annie and the goats spend most of their day inside the barn and pick the greener grass from under the trees at twilight.

The Valley's world is changing, going from semi-tropical to arid over a matter of but a few years. Will we see the end of our lush vegetation? What is it that we must to do keep our plants alive and, yet, to save water? I'm willing to do it— but in the meantime, I intend to continue to say a prayer every night, to thank God for the privilege of living in this glorious Valley of ours, and, please, God, send lots and lots of rain. (Soon)

Tears

Of course, I cried. I'm not superwoman, you know. They weren't tears from the heart; they were tears from the soul. The anger, the frustration tears that almost every woman is reduced to at some time in her life. (Don't get me wrong, we hate it, we don't want it and we fight it like tigers, but they prevail.) So with tear filled eyes and quavering voice, I reiterated my position– "This is not right! I think that this will cause many problems!" and again, my pleas fall upon deaf ears. Men, they just don't get it! Women get angry and they sniffle. Don't take it personal, guys; just feel that it is the gentle rain before the storm. This teary-eyed frustration is not to be confused with teary-eyed hurt. Uh uh– not the same, not the same, at all. If all things proceed at the same rate, you can then expect the containment of the tears then the silence. This is a brief situation, and it doesn't bode well for the "other guy".

Next stage, the ragged voice, no longer filled with tears, but kind of rasping and hostile– (half-hostile *because* of the tears)– and ready to come to terms with whatever the problem. The voice now rising and falling with frustration– the "just listen to me for one minute" voice– the "please, before I lose control and whap you with my briefcase!" voice.

And, **finally,** the take charge– "That's it!" "Just stop, give me a chance to speak, YOU listen for one minute, and THEN give me your critique– after you hear the FULL story". (Ladies, have you noticed that when you are in an argument situation, you are only allowed to give one half of your sentences— they either finish them for you or dispute them before you have ever even finalized them in your mind? Ohhhh, I hate that.

My favorite "rejection to theory" mode is that after I say eight words *toward* my real idea, my friend already has his scrawny little hand up, directed in the general area of my face, in a traffic cop "Stop" position. So that, before I get my say (slow and, maybe, formative as it might be) he is already embarking on his own scenario. Many times, was my idea to be heard in its entirety, it is the same as his— maybe a variation of his— perhaps totally different, but a logical idea none the less.

Now, don't get me wrong— this is not an every day occurrence— just one that happens every once in a while. (Enough to leave those of us who crave justice to give warning.) We hate it that we spring to tears when angered. Those unwanted tears make us feel, perhaps, out of control– vulnerable.

I find that I am in these situations *mostly* when I have been left "out of the loop" on some project or item— when I am trying to understand what has happened (or is happening) and I struggle to get up to speed. That's when the questions surface and the tentative thoughts and ideas arise. The opportunity for those frustration tears to well up is just around the corner at this point, and we dread enduring the stop sign hands and the "no no— you just aren't following" gestures and we go primitive— tears.

God gave the sexes some very different characteristics and although I understand that even men get the stop sign hand occasionally, as well as those negative side to side finger motions (as in "tsk tsk"). I wonder how they handle it. No tears, that's for certain. Although, I would love to see a Nate Newton-sized paw strike out and grab that stop sign hand someday, in my heart, I doubt if that day will come. Heck, I might just have to do it myself.

God Bless America

I didn't want to go– honest, I just plain didn't want to go. After all, it was NYPD Blue night and I was leaving town the next day and I don't go out at night– and and and - You get the picture, right? I didn't want to go.

Larry Pressler (Director of McAllen Parks & Recreation) sent the Commissioners tickets to go to the 'Town Band's Symphonic Orchestra'. Then he _called_ - You **are** coming to the Town Band tonight, aren't you?"– I listed the above reasons and sniveled– "Larry, you know I don't like to go out at night". He's a tough taskmaster, and I finally acquiesced– "Ok, ok but I'm leaving at the Intermission, alright?"

My winter visitor friends, Dick and Betty, from Lincoln, Nebraska, were willing accomplices as we plotted to go - but to vanish at the Intermission. We couched our "escape" plan with "we really like the music, and would really love to stay, however, we (see above)". We were less than an enthusiastic group plodding into the McAllen Civic Center on Tuesday night. Larry, good to his word, had set aside seats for the Commissioners; Dick, Betty and I sat dutifully front and center.

The first song literally exploded onto the stage - THE STAR SPANGLED BANNER– sung by Matias Garcia, and we were goners. The man's clear voice rang through the rafters of our old auditorium while the audience stood with hands on hearts and tears in eyes. We no longer remained hostage to our escape plans, but sat, mesmerized through the first half of the concert. The flutes, the horns, the tinkling things and the great gold tuba— and bunches of musical instruments emitting sounds that flowed effortlessness together, caused us to clap 'til our little hands were sore.

The McAllen Symphonic Band dedicated a march to the City of McAllen— it was especially commissioned to commemorate the 25th Anniversary of the McAllen Town Band Assoc. Thus began the second half of the program. The Wizard of Oz, the St. Louis Blues, and the Pink Panther followed.

Ok, so I'll admit it, I really didn't think they could outdo what they had already done, when they began the **Armed Forces Salute**. It was a medley of service songs, from Anchors Aweigh to the Caissons are Rolling Along and at the onset of each segment, the veterans in the audience stood— they stood to *their* song, the song that addressed *their* branch. As the Band played and the men and women kept standing, I realized that, overhead; the spotlights were red, white and blue, and the gentle lights reflected off of a hundred silver heads, the heads of proud veterans, who stood out of respect to their branch of the Armed Forces. I felt a fierce kind of pride, pride in America and a special kind of pride in MY City of McAllen for enabling a function like this to be held for folks like me.

The ladies and gentlemen of the Orchestra were attired in tuxedos, but the audience was laid back, pretty much in denim and casual wear. It really didn't matter the dress of either participant, however, as we were all caught up in an evenings' fantasy— a fantasy born out of artisans who play their instruments from the heart, and an audience who frankly appreciated every note and every sound.

With the caissons rolling "aweigh" and the Marines seeking a few good men, we were prepared to sing along with the maestro "American the Beautiful"— for the grand finale. That just didn't happen. We had a special narrator who told us about the song, the woman who wrote it, and why. He explained each verse as our Matias Garcia sang it. When the gigantic American Flag slowly lowered behind the Orchestra, the applause was deafening. What a wonderful evening— thanks to the McAllen Symphonic Band! You say you're doing your Christmas Show on December 15? I'll be the one in the front row, glad to be out at night!

Thanks Larry, I needed that!

Kaleidoscope Evening

It's just been one of those lazy South Texas weekends, and as I think back across the kaleidoscope of my past three days I laugh out loud. What began as the usual "gee, what should I do with myself?" weekend, turned into a "how do I duplicate it?" weekend.

Friends play such an important part in our lives, and when multiple friends and multiple activities occupy the waking hours of a little old lady such as me, life is indeed good. When a friend came in from San Antonio, I was delighted! We decided to do the homebody thing, and we talked and walked and told each other stories of other lives and other days. Learning more about each other and learning, perhaps, a bit more about ourselves. Isn't it strange how new friends can lure a person right into some boring story about something that happened 30 years ago? The laughs that you had back then suddenly become the laughs of today, and while weaving the tapestry of your earlier life, you suddenly realize that *these* days, today and tomorrow, will be as funny and interesting (or not) in the future as we now feel yesterdays stories are.

Actually, let me begin the weekend early morning on Thursday, when I stepped to the diving board (to do my early morning scanning of the yard, birds, and miscellaneous animals) and stood resolutely, but quickly, I must admit) on my glasses. Now, how in the World would a thing like that happen? By the time evening fell, I had bumped into the nightstand, burned an egg, and bread-machined a small tough loaf of bread. I thought to my self, "Scheesh— it's just going to be another one of "those" days". Then my friend arrived. I regaled him with stories of broken glasses and burned eggs and a fresh "day-old" loaf of bread, and our laughter washed it all away. (And we ate the bread anyway!)

Friday was once again upon us and I had the opportunity to stop by the Hospital and see Jennifer and Danny's new baby. Wow, how can that much baby fit into such a little stomach area? He looked much like a little old man, with Danny's lips, but pretty cute anyhow! When my pals, the Arriaga's, invited me to join them at the Lincoln Day Dinner that evening, I joined up and we discussed (and cussed) politics and elections and party food and, of course, Aggies. Why Aggies? You always have to discuss Aggies when you are with the family Arriaga. It's the law...

Late Friday evening finds me, again, sitting in the back yard, listening to birdcalls and seeing the clouds rush by overhead. A feeling of peacefulness fills me and I realize how much this Rio Grande Valley means to me. The flowers and the trees, the bird sounds and the scent of the orange blossoms wafting across the yard all mean McAllen to me.

Life is good.

Play Ball!

It was early of a morning when I heard Bob growl from the end of the bed. A low, quiet growl– nothing fancy– just "grrrrrrrrrr" very quietly. It's an event when Bob growls, and I tuned my keen ears into the night darkness of the early morning. Then I could hear it, a high, keening whistle sound– not loud, but audible, none the less.

Slipping from beneath the covers, I moved quietly to the end of the bed, giving Bob a pat on the head on the way. Whistle– whistle– I could still hear the faint whistle. Quietly now, to the burglar alarm which showed all systems under control. Whistle, whistle– perhaps a door is ajar, I sneak through the house, bed-head disheveled and nightshirt rumpled, carrying a heavy flashlight by now, cautiously, carefully.

The whistle becomes steadily softer away from the bedroom, and as I wind my way back to my room the whistle becomes more pronounced. It's dark (they say always darkest before the dawn, right?) and I feel my way along the walls and stand, once again at the foot of the bed. The light on my little clock radio beams out 4:15 and I wonder if the sound doesn't emanate from the clock. I pull the plug– whistle whistle– I am on my knees now, listening, ear pressed to bed, then to nightstand. The nightstand is the culprit and I open the drawer carefully, ever so carefully. Whistle whistle– loud now– and as I start moving items around in the drawer it grows ever louder.

The, without warning, a tinny version of "Take Me Out To The Ballgame" whistles out from a very small, very clever pin that I got when I went with Parks and Recreation to recruit the Girls Softball Games to McAllen. What prompted the sudden outburst, the happy song, I will never know, but I am certainly viewing that pin with a whole new attitude.

Perhaps the Edinburg Roadrunners are in need of a perfectly good middle aged lady who knows all the words (and a perfectly good tinny version) of Take Me Out To The Ballgame… PLLLLLAAAAAYYYYY BAAAALLLLLL (but not at 4:15 AM– ok?)

Heroes

During a flurry of channel switching the other evening, as I flashed by The Wonder Years, Kevin Arnold said something so profound, that I was inspired to commit it to memory: "Every kid needs to be a hero once in his life!" (This was after a frantic Little League game and HE made the crucial home run and was carried around on the other player's shoulders.)s

Expanding on THAT theory, we must assume that everyone needs to be a hero at least once in their life. But to define "hero" is the difficult part.

It's easy for me to recall the time when my Tracy was probably in 9th grade -(basketball WAS her life) and during the last seconds of an extremely close game, ("they" were one point ahead of us) she was fouled, personally, and stood, resolutely, alone, in the middle of the box, to shoot two free throws. The opposing team was catcalling from the other side, and our side sat, with hearts in mouths, silent as ghosts. I wondered then as I wonder now how she kept her hands from shaking as she shot - the first shot - IN!! And amidst the shrieking from the audience, sunk the second shot with nary a backward glance. A hero if I ever saw one!

Fifteen years later, my chum, sidekick and neighbor, Robin Moore, an eighth grader, leaps from the safety of her inner tube in the swirling Guadeloupe River to hold her non-swimming middle aged friend's head above water until rescuers arrive. Without Robin's clear thinking and unselfish devotion, I would, at this writing, be just one more statistic in the Saga of mighty Guadelupe. Robin Moore, a hero if I ever saw one!

But in looking around in my day to day adventures, I find heroes at every turn and in the strangest of places. The other morning at the Donut Shop, I saw a regular customer who hadn't been in for many weeks. Immediately accosting her, I demanded to know where she had been and what she had been doing to be away for such a long time. She said she had been doing what she usually does in the summer - teaching migrant children in Wisconsin. Bertha Guerra, teacher from Roosevelt School - hero!!

Amalia Molina from our own Chamber of Commerce moved Heaven and Earth to see that a child who was kidnapped by a family member and taken into Mexico was returned to his parents. My kind of hero!

I wonder about the unsung heroes who stand at the School crossings - the Moms and the Dads who stand out there in the heat, rain and wind. Does anyone ever tell them what a truly good thing that they are doing? Does anyone really realize how much time and effort they spend? THEY are heroes in my book.

My mom was a hero. She just didn't know it. By the time that I figured it out, it was toward the end of her life and I couldn't convince her of it! She had been the kind of mom who baked cookies and kept the house immaculate and adored my dad. She was raised in the slums of Omaha, Nebraska, the oldest of 9 children. She quit school in 8th grade to go to work to recover the income lost when her 37-year-old father died.

Some 50 years later when her husband, my father, died, she dived into his little Auto Parts and Paint business and increased the business threefold in the ten years before she died. My mom - hiding her light under that proverbial bushel basket all those years. Had we but known the potential that lurked beneath that cake baking, pork chop dusting, apron covered exterior! My mom, obviously, was a hero at both ends of her life. I miss my hero - my mom...

So if there's a hero in your life, and you haven't told them yet - please do it. You'll both be the better for it.

Heroes don't have to be told, I'm told, but go out on a limb - tell 'em..

Success Story

For me to write a column about being a woman in business, politics or charity work, I will have to take you back to South Dakota, some 25 years ago. Married, working full time as a secretary, living on a farm, mowing and baling hay, raising a few horses and cattle in our spare time (namely before work, after work and on weekends) life was fun, but hard. My vision of "success" (in some far off point in my life) was to be able to pay cash for a horse! The thought was farfetched, I knew, but hope springs eternal.

So, I find being "successful" a lot more complicated than I originally thought. The raising of a child who becomes a useful member of society, the respect of your peers, the ability to make a difference in your community, peace of mind, good health...These are the ingredients of success..

While I always felt that my most successful "project" was raising my daughter, Tracy, I now know it to be true. I was a single parent from the time she was 7 and she was a constant source of pride to me. She graduated from McHi in the Top 25. She played first string basketball all through High School. (I was "Team Mom" and never missed a game.) She graduated from SMU in 1986 and works in the Embassy in Athens as one of the few female Diplomats for the State Department. While she is my success story, she is her own success story as well.

City Commission? Being McAllen's first female City Commissioner probably doesn't have one thing to do with the fact that it is the most difficult, the most time consuming, and most definitely, the most frustrating job I have ever tackled. We have 92,000 citizen bosses, one extremely strong Mayor, and three other commissioners as different as night and day. Put five leaders, five different backgrounds, opinions and thoughts, you have - I guess- just what it's suppose to be - a democracy.

We've had our bad times during my tour of duty, but we've all done what we thought was best for the community. We have been accessible to citizens, we've helped and we've cared. Yes, this position has been a unique experience in my life - while some sometimes not as fulfilling as "paying cash for a horse" definitely more rewarding in the long haul.

Women are making a difference out there, not only in organizations, and on Boards, but on an on going basis of helping other women. I could name a dozen that give 110% to helping make this City a better for women to excel. I hope that I am considered one of those women who help other women, what a grand success THAT would be.

Family

The compact "family" of an only child demands very little. Our little family was probably as crazy and unscheduled as anyone's. We laughed a lot, my mom, my dad and me. My dad ran the show, and mom and I were just along for the ride, we never questioned his ability to determine the course of our lives, he just did.

These stories are real and, believe me; I have included anything and everything that would cause embarrassment to any of my family– they are my own treasures– and they would laugh with me at some of the antics.

My only sadness is that my mom isn't alive to read and enjoy *her* stories. My dad would scoff at the idea that he actually built the boat in the dining room, but would laugh and snicker later when alone.

My family– I miss them.

The Child Brigade

I was an ill child, a scrawny, knobby-kneed child with sallow complexion and dark, deep-set eyes... It was a life filled with tests and needles and doctors. Bronchial pneumonia at four, raging fever and delirious with measles at five, at six, ruptured appendix removed. One obstacle would pass and another would surface.

When Rheumatic fever was at its zenith, I, of course, spent a year in the Denver Children's Hospital battling the disease with a host of other "warriors" in bed after bed there in the pediatrics ward. Visiting days were twice a week and the "child brigade" waited for parents with sullen faces and reports of lousy oatmeal and soggy toast and nurses who couldn't braid or comb out a girl's tangled hair. Our parents stood, in white caps and gowns, masks across faces, somberly assessing and evaluating the reports. Parent days usually brought about many gifts and, for me, books. The parents left saddened and the children (me included) cried piteously when we saw the last of the white gowns fluttering down the hall. When I finally went home, I was weakened and unable to play outside,

I took my council in books. The couch was my sanctuary where watching the other children sledding down the hill in front of the house, left me grieving for the loss of my childhood. I retreated further and further into the "Child's Garden of Verses" and "The Boxcar Children", among others, and I realized that those friendly pages would never tell if you were scrawny or ill.

Mother was a saint who had carried tray after tray to me over those years - surprises of bright cherry Jell-O with bananas or, for breakfast, French toast with the crusts cut off. I was a snarling, ungrateful sick kid with a real attitude problem - I did, however, have infrequent bouts of niceness, but didn't appreciate Mom nearly as much as I should have... She sat by my bed, most evenings, reading to me - poems and adventure stories and promising me that most stories had happy endings, and I would soon be back out playing. In retrospect, my illness was a time of learning for me - learning of children who play in cherry trees and heroic dogs that come home again and again; horses that pull junk carts and are rescued and eventually win the Kentucky Derby. I read and I dreamed and I believed and I became well. In the decades since I was that ill child, my health has been so blatantly good, that I have shivered over my friends' health woes and wondered if all of my illnesses lay behind me.

Dr. Bieker told me that my eyes had changed, for the worse, by double, in just five days, I was stunned - what? Why? After numerous blood tests and frantic denials, lo and behold, it was diagnosed as Diabetes. Once again to be cast among the needles and doctors, I was frightened and unknowledgeable about the disease. That was a few weeks ago and it felt as though only I was without knowledge on Diabetes.

Immediately I was sent off to counseling - diet and instruction - do's and don'ts - pills and admonitions. Changing of existing medication and stacks of information. I'm reading about sugars and tingling toes and I am believing and dreaming and feeling that I will soon become well.

I only wish I had been more understanding when my own father suddenly had Diabetes appear when he was my age, and that I would see my mom round the corner, carrying a tray with some of that bright cherry Jell-O and a cup of tea and cinnamon toast (with the crust cut off..) Heck, I just wish she would come sit by my bed and tell me that all stories have happy endings and I will soon be back out to play.

A Miserable Merry Christmas

It wasn't necessarily an unusual story, I had actually read one like it myself (it had been my favorite Christmas Story) - an unknown, I now know, author, and a story of a little boy who wanted nothing but a pony for Christmas. If he couldn't have a pony, he wanted nothing at all. He planned and he worked hard, cleaning the shed behind his house and filling the floor of it with golden straw, waiting Christmas morning...

Lo and behold, when Christmas morning arrived, there were no gifts beneath the tree for the little boy and no pony as well. With brimming eyes, he sat on the front porch, knowing that he, and only he, had set down the rules and had to live with them. His dad and mom were pacing, giving nervous glances up the road and at each other. Finally, mid afternoon, (after breaking my little heart several more times, as he lay sobbing there in the stall on the golden straw) he sees a strange sight coming up his road - a fine pony, being ridden by a lanky man, feet almost touching the ground. As he approached, he called out to the boy "Do you know where the Smith's live? I was supposed to deliver this pony to their boy, Tom, at 6 am this morning and I have been lost." Needless to say, the rest is stuff from which Christmas stories are made and boy and pony lived, I believed (and believe) happily ever after.

As a horse crazy little girl, who had read "The Miserable Merry Christmas" (above) about 20 times in her lifetime, I, too, was bound and determined to have my very own horse for Christmas. It was in September, I had just passed my eleventh birthday and threw down the gauntlet to my parents - I want a horse for Christmas, and if I can't have one, I don't want anything.

"A horse? Here in Kansas City?" dad said. (We lived on the outskirts of Kansas City, Missouri...) "Sure, honey, you find a place to keep a horse, we'll see what we can do." (He felt safe with this particular obstacle, and grinned confidently behind his newspaper...) However, no challenge is too great for a kid having to have her very own horse, and I began canvassing the farms beyond our little suburb. The reclusive farmer at the end of our street (called "Farmer Brown" by the irreverent adults in the neighborhood) lived in a patched up old house with falling down out buildings and lots and lots of dogs. We kids were half afraid of him (we had seen him in the fields in his bib overalls, carrying a stick, which, of course, labeled him as crazy to us.) but courage comes naturally to a little girl wanting her very own horse, and I went calling on Farmer Brown.

Admittedly, I skirted the area many times before I made my move. With heart in throat, I approached him there in the barnyard - dogs were barking and cats circled his legs as he was filling pans and tins with fresh milk. I must have looked as insignificant as I felt, and my voice barely registered as I mumbled "Farmer Brown?" He stood staring at me, "Farmer Brown"?? he bellowed! He then started laughing and said "Well, that's just good enough." I wrestled with the dogs and petted the cats and stared at the big coffee-with-cream colored cow and Farmer Brown and I began a friendship that lasted a lifetime...

It was weeks later, after the novelty of being friends with an adult, an old adult at that, had worn off, that I broached the subject of my Christmas wish of having a horse. I found that he actually had an old horse himself - a plow horse that had seen much action in his day -and had been dispatched to a "better place" just recently - and he concurred, that an animal lover such as me *should* have her very own horse.

He volunteered to come to visit with dad, and I tried to do the introductions with fidgety ineptitude, but Farmer Brown himself stepped in and introduced himself "My name's A.C. Dehart, I'm a friend of Phyllis'" he said. I, of course, reeled back in horror - I had been calling him "Farmer Brown" - to his face, yet, for these many weeks. How stupid he must have thought me, how rude... But as he continued his visit with dad, "Phyllis calls me Farmer Brown, why don't you just do the same."

The ad was placed in the newspaper that very next day "Wanted: horse suitable for eleven-year-old girl", etc. etc." We traveled many miles before we found the *perfect* horse for an eleven-year-old girl.

Christmas afternoon, as dusk was falling, and my heart was almost breaking, up the street drove a beat up old truck, pulling a beat up old trailer and silhouetted there, in the evening sky, I could see the alert head of my very own horse. As we unloaded her, the neighbors all turned on their porch lights and my horse and I walked down the lighted pathway to Farmer Brown's place, where a stall waited with golden straw on the floor, I, too, had had the most miserable, yet Merriest Christmas of them all.

I Remember Roy

Remembering Roy Rogers is rather like remembering your blanket when you were a child - it, and he, were always there for you. The one intimate recollection that I have of Roy was when I was— golly, I must have been, six years old. He had his very own radio program; it was late of an evening, and I was privileged to get to listen to his program in my mom's room. Dad was usually out of town on the night Roy made his late night visit into my folks' bedroom. So mom and I would sit importantly up against the headboard of the bed, whispering and giggling until the program came on, then to raptly listen to each word.

Needless to say, he was my personal hero, and now, in retrospect, I wonder if he wasn't my mom's hero as well. The night I remember so vividly, was a night of toothpicks and home fries and ketchup and big glasses of chocolate milk. Mom was great at making things seem fun and grown up— and to lie in bed and eat home fries with toothpicks and dunk them into the fiery red ketchup was truly life in the fast lane for me. We, of course, were into Ovaltine and she had mixed some up in a large glass container, with a handy little whipper that you plunged up and down. So it was with frothy glasses of chocolate Ovaltine and home fried potatoes that we learned the news.

Roy had been seen holding hands with Dale Evans! I wasn't quite certain how that actually affected *me*, but mother's outcry convinced me that it boded a certain amount of harm to my on-going relationship with him. Mom said that she had read in *The Ladies Home Journal* that Roy and Dale were a "number" and I quizzed her about the possible effects to Roy and to all of "us", his fans. She didn't seem to know, but was scandalized about the inappropriateness of his handholding right there at the table in the cafeteria at the studio.

I tried to visualize the incident— the tablecloth (the only really nice place we went to eat had red and white tablecloths) had to be red and white and their hands going beneath the cloth to touch and, even linger. Did he have on his white hat during this intimate moment? How could someone else see this incident? Who exactly WAS Dale Evans? Did she deserve him?

Mom said that the magazine article told that she had been married before— or was it that he had? Whatever the case, we grimly speared our home fries and plunged them into the ketchup. A major concern, to me, was that would he be able to keep Trigger AND have a woman in his life.

There are many questions that a six-year-old girl can ask, and I'm certain that mom's ears were ringing before that night was over.

The trauma of that evening, even now, allows me to revisit that bedroom again and again. The furniture was light colored wood, and there were table lamps on each side of the bed, and the warm glow of the lamps made the bedroom a fairyland for us. The warmth of the lamp's glow was nothing compared to the warmth of the mom and daughter relationship that night. I wasn't just a kid that night; I was a participant in a very special occasion. Roy Rogers had a girlfriend and I thought I was the first to know.

Sure, I remember Roy. He was the good guy; he wore the white hat and caught the bad guys. He rode the amazing Trigger and he fell in love and got married and lived happily ever after.

My Grandmother's Robe

My Grandmother was buried in a white satin bathrobe with a dragon breathing red satin fire on the back. Well, you see, it's kind of a long story about my grandmother....

Grandmother Rieger came to visit my parents, (speaking very little English and a lot of German) when mom was pregnant with me. Mom said she was kind of suspicious when grandma showed up with her bed and feather comforter and three or four trunks of clothing that year, but she just never imagined that she would stay forever. Grandma was kind of the bad news and the good news. She loved to work - she cleaned, she washed and she ironed as though she was born to it. While I believe that mom was happy to have someone working about the house, I also imagine that she wanted to do it herself. At any rate, it was great for me - no babysitters, no doing dishes, no ironing in my little growing up lifetime.

The bad news, however, was when we moved to a new City, (we moved frequently, as my dad worked for the Government), grandma would hit the bricks - going from door to door, offering her services for ironing, washing, and the like. Mom was always embarrassed, but Dad said that a little honest work never hurt anyone. Grandma Rieger was also a Jehovah's Witness, and when she would knock at those strange new doors and offer her services, she would also offer the services of her Jehovah and hand them a publication and a pep talk.

She was a picture, my grandmother! She was square of build, not particularly tall; her long, long, grey hair (she called it "them hairs") was twisted severely into a bun at the back of her head. She always wore a hat, usually with a flower on the front or side, her sides were firmly corseted, sturdy black shoes and several pairs of heavy cotton stockings (far be it that ANYONE view any portion of her actual body) and a dark dress always down to mid calf.

I see her in my minds eye today as I saw her then, this wonderful square little old lady, standing on the street corner, rain or shine, snow or heat, with her canvas bag of "Awake" magazines (Jehovah's Witness publication) over her shoulder, and her humble attempts (and oft time successes) to convert passers-by.

But, now back to the white satin bathrobe. When Cousin Harold was in Korea, he sent all of us items of clothing from the Far East - Grandmother's white satin bathrobe with the dragon breathing fire on the back brought about gasps of fear from mom, dad and me. We got sort of a community box of stuff and each item was carefully tagged with our names - and sure enough, there was grandma's name on the bathrobe. Grandma's idea of "colorful" was a muted pink or yellow flower on her hat and dark green was as colorful as her wardrobe ever became. So it was with a good deal of trepidation that we took the robe to grandma. We discussed the shock she would suffer from this totally inappropriate gift, the hurt she would endure from cousin Harold's insensitivity to her needs. So, when it was presented to her and she teared up, we were not surprised! Poor thing! Then, lo and behold, she cradled it like a baby and clutched it to her ample bosom. She folded the large white satin arms back to expose a red satin underside and she patted and oooohhh and aaaahhhh'ed and declared it was, by far, the finest and most beautiful thing she had ever owned and she wanted to be buried in it.

Her wish came true some 10 years later, and I smile to think of her in her casket, carefully coifed, them hairs severely pulled back in a bun, her serene face (that never saw makeup) smiling up from the folds of that white satin bathrobe with the red satin lining and, of course, the fire breathing dragon on the back.

While she was somewhat a conservative dresser here on Earth, I imagine her to be a very colorful member of the Citizenry in Heaven.

Dad Said It Was Easy

The anti-smoking crusade is certainly (if you'll pardon the expression) a burning issue with business owners and Elected Officials these days. Far be it from me to take this all lightly - as a person who tried diligently in her youth to smoke (thinking that I would become instantly thin) to a person in mid-life who gets a headache sitting next to a smoker. I know, first hand that smoke kills, my dad, Fritz, was a smoker - a lifetime smoker, and, in the end, a deathbed smoker as well.

I remember dad, during WW2, taking the "tin foil" we called it, from his cigarette packs and saving it in neat packages to sell or to give (I can't recall) to the War effort. Early of a morning I would hear him waking - he had a particular "cough-a-hoffa" would alert me that he was about to get up and have a cup of coffee and that all important cigarette.

Throughout childhood, I can recall seeing his face set in fierce concentration, one eye squinting to avoid the smoke from the "ciggie" hanging in the corner of his mouth. He was a creator, he built, he envisioned, he planned and drew out those plans on napkins and yellow lined sheets, to later transform our living area into some construction war-zone. A designer kitchen with polished hand-made cabinets and tabletops could mysteriously appear and would draw rave reviews from the neighbors. He would stand proudly aside, cigarette burning brightly between his yellowed fingers, accepting the praise as his due. When he built his boat in the dining room, the smoke, the sawdust and debris kept ALL of us coughing - until it was finished. Of course, THAT particular time, the neighbors came in to see how the finished product was to be REMOVED from the dining room. - With ciggie clenched firmly between his teeth, he boldly proclaimed "no problem" and removed a portion of the outside wall - to be replaced at a later date when the boat was safely in the water.

The 16 MM films that I have of our vacation times and his hunting and fishing days, the cigarette was ever present. He said it was easy to quit smoking - that he had done it dozens of times. He was ready to admit that it was a bad habit, but he had no idea how really bad it was until his already husky voice became huskier and then quiet and was then gone. The news was an affront to him - cancer? Unheard of in that day and time - yet when the gurney came back with Dad, his 6' frame seemed smaller, and his 200+ pounds seemed lighter - and his throat was a gaping wound with his voice box gone. He never really recovered to his old swaggering, devil may care ways - the ever present cigarette was replaced with the vibrating voice box that he pressed, to his throat, to speak. He hated the disease and he hated his condition and pretty much hated his life after that - but he never once said, to our amazement, that he hated the dreaded cigarette.

My amazing dad, builder, creator, adventurer, rogue, dreamer, brought to reality by a mere cigarette.

Valentine Mom

Valentine's Day was my mom's Birthday; however, she was *our* Valentine year around. She was always there, apron tied neatly in back, cookie sheets either going into or out of the oven, when I came home from school - the frosty glass of milk waiting. She regaled my school chums and I by reading to us after school - I remember, especially, when The Green Grass of Wyoming came out in the newspaper - continued every day. We would file into the "spare" bedroom and assume our positions. Mom, of course, reading from the straight back chair, and my friends and I sprawled hither and yon upon bed and floor, glasses of milk in hand, and plate of cookies within reach. The cowboy tale kept us raptly attentive and our mutual love of horses caused us to whisper of having our own someday soon.

Mom was raised in the slums of Omaha, Nebraska, the oldest of 9 children, the daughter of a tubercular father and an ill mother. She said she only remembered one of the two sets of twins that died - they lay "in state" in their living room, in shoe boxes, and when people went in to pay their respects, it was so cold that she could see their breath. When her dad died at age 39, she quit school to go to work. During the day she worked in a factory, and in the evenings as a maid to some Polish neighbors - she said she thought, at that time, that they were terribly rich, as they always had a pot of soup simmering on the stove. She said she was actually happier then than any time she could remember in her childhood - they could make ends meet and you could no longer see "your breath in the living room".

She was a hell-raiser, as a girl, she said, and she kept me intrigued as she sat by the side of my bed in the evening telling me stories of her youth. Her recollections were of violent childhood pranks between her and her brothers - to include her throwing a hatchet at my uncle Dick and having it land on the front of the chair rung where he was hiding. She said that she tortured her younger brother, my uncle Dean, with stories of hideous mutants and creatures that would crawl in from the river that lay but a distance from their house. My only (now) living uncle, my uncle Gene, fled from the house when he was 15 to join the NAVY, and never really returned home.

Grandmother, a skinny, nervous soul was sick most of the time, and the five children of the house plagued her no end. Mother said that grandmother really wasn't mean spirited, but life had simply dealt her too many blows. Having her husband die so young left her to her own devices, and with no skills, she was an old woman at 40, body crippled with arthritis; mind crippled with bitterness. It was a different World then, and they remained captive to their poverty; there in that rickety old house, with the outdoor toilet, next to the river and under the Viaduct.

Life back then, though hard and colorless, did not keep mom from being sentimental and a died-in-the-wool romantic. She said she was born on Valentines Day in the year 1913, and every year, we dutifully bought her the most colorful Valentines/Birthday cards - sometimes they were a combination of BOTH days. We dragged home heart shaped boxes of candy and made a tradition of Mom being our very own sweetheart on a daily basis. After all, she WAS born on Valentines Day.

My mom, a singer of songs and a teller of tales; a pork chop dusting, cookie baking romantic from a not so romantic time. But could you expect less from a Valentine Girl?

When she died, I happened upon her birth certificate, and laughed aloud when I found that my romantic, sweetheart of a Mom was born on February 13, not February 14. A harmless, romantic, little white lie that lasted 75 years... I miss my mom, my hero, my Valentine

Happy Mother's Day, Mom.

Family Affairs

I am spending more time than usual in front of the personal "rogues gallery" in my bedroom here lately. My mom graces many frames and I can't help but grin at the picture of mom and me (I must have been four or five old) - she is wearing (honest!) a lace gizmo on her head that looks like one of those lace things that go under lamp. I actually remember my rakish dad standing off and gazing at her with wonder - "Kate, do you know that you a doily on your head?" She was not pleased with the criticism and declared that SHE thought it looked just perfect. She hated the picture, but loved the hat - an ode to her crocheting prowess...

Dad always looked like dad in his pictures. He seemed to be pleased with the outcome - never once to mutter that he "just didn't look right". He was without guile and was content to be and look like himself. He was a big, thick shouldered guy, a few locks of hair across his size 7 3/4 head and the fringe encircling that. He normally had a nice, neat pencil line mustache that provoked no notice at all. Then one year he simply went nuts! I actually think it was to aggravate mom; he grew the BIG mustache - he waxed the ends and they were curled in a (1) flashy snail look or (2) stuck out with the ends looking remarkably like the ends of shoe strings. Mom would narrow her eyes at him as he would stand in doorway grinning. She tried not to encourage him in "silliness" and it tickled him no end. Early of a morning as Mom and I waited breakfast for dad (he was readying himself for the days work) - we heard a scream from down the hallway. Mom leaped to her feet and stood at the end of the hall - "Are OK, Fritz?" A muttered "yeh, yeh" calmed her and she, drinking her coffee, wondering what calamity had dad encountered there in the bathroom. He appeared, his white "hanky" clutched to his upper lip; he was bloody, but un-daunted as he explained that he had accidentally caught the end of his "stache" in his electric razor and "dammed near ripped my lip off!".

Wish that I could tell you that compassion ran as deep as our love in my family, but I can't. Mother and I got hysterical - pointing - laughing - offering suggestions "whack the other side off, too!" "be a trend setter - only have ONE shoe lace". He ultimately cut the side off and went back to his neat, nice no one will mustache.

We were a traveling family, dad being a Government man; we could pack up and move at the drop of a hat. One particularly memorable trip had us speeding from Colorado to Des Moines, Iowa. We ALWAYS sped from one location to the other. My dad, while a good driver, brooked no interference from mom or me while "on the road". We were simply passengers on this flight, and we followed all of the rules. Dad's job, of course, was to get us to destination as fast as possible - mind always racing to the next stop or final destination. We carried junk food with us, so the only scheduled stops were for gas. We had to coordinate our restroom stops with gas stops - period. It was a rainy, cool morning when we made our first stop. I, sleeping in the backseat, vaguely heard the doors opening and closing, but when we resumed our flight down the highway I snuggled back under my blanket. I roused up some to 15 minutes later and leaned over the seat to inquire of dad - "Where's mom?"

When we got back to the service station, there was mom – fit to be tied, primly sitting on the bench in front, her sweater clutched about her shoulders. She didn't say a word, marched up to the car, got in and stared directly out front window. Dad reared back against the driver side; I actually believe he started to apologize, but what started off as a grin, began to build and finally he was laughing and wiping his eyes and sputtering and lo and behold, before long, she, too, was laughing and wiping. I stared, dumbfounded, for a moment or so and then joined in the fun. Parents didn't always make sense to me, but somehow, it really didn't matter all that much.

Uncle Bud

Uncle Bud was probably 6'2" in his stocking feet, but dressed in his usual "gitup" of boots and cowboy hat– he seemed to be taller than a tree. He was a doorway full, our uncle Bud, from the raven black hair combed straight back from his brow to the toes of his dusty boots, uncle Bud was a "hand" (as we called 'em in those days).

Uncle Bud ranched in Buffalo, South Dakota, with Aunt Florence and their three kids, 35 years ago. It was a hard country - long dry summers could and would be followed by harsh winters and the daily tolls that just plain life took, was incredible. It just never seemed to bother Uncle Bud, his eyes were brimming with laughter and he usually had some sort of a grin on his face. He could repair the tractor with the same ease he roped the toughest steer and moving cattle when it was 30 degrees below zero just brought out that extra pair of long johns. He never complained, but lived life as though every day was his last.

When Uncle Bud got sick that summer we all were stunned - sick? Uncle Bud sick? Unheard of - but true. When the first report came in - a reaction to cattle spray (we all envisioned the dust filled corral, milling cattle, and Uncle Bud adjusting the spray on the rig) - it made sense -sort of - but that report was immediately followed by another - leukemia - final stages. We were devastated! Not Uncle Bud - he was angry - hey! He was only 50+- and he had a lot of "stuff" to do! When he and his son, Donny won the team roping at Ekalaka, Montana, on Sunday, who could imagine that the following Saturday, we would be filing into the little Church on Main Street in Buffalo, South Dakota, to pay our last respects?

It was a windy, overcast day, and the ranchers and cowboys came from miles around to show their respect for Uncle Bud - the Church was filled to capacity and the mourners stood in the dusty wind-swept street, hats in hands. The casket was adorned with a blanket of white carnations with his brand emblazoned across the front in red carnations - bar B bar.

The family burial plot was in the horse pasture, on the other side of the ranch. After the Church service the Limo carrying Uncle Bud led a parade of two or three miles of cars and pickup trucks down the seven miles to the turn off and another three miles down the dusty trail of a road, past the ranch, to the horse pasture. When the Limo stopped for the driver to open the gate, I turned around and stared through the swirling dust at headlights reaching back as far as I could see and angry skies tumbling overhead.

Here in the horse pasture, not in my wildest imagination would I have ever imagined the sight that was upon us. Racing from beyond some ledge, from around some hill, came the horses - and for one moment, the sun blazed with a fierceness that turned the stallion's coat to fire. Baldy, Uncle Bud's stallion - ears straining, nostrils flaring, was leading mares and colts, surging, in a seemingly well-planned drill, between the Hearse and the rest of the cars. They fanned away to stand motionless on a nearby hill, and then disappeared into the, once again, gloom.

Cars stopped and doors flew open when we arrived at the cemetery - the only one who wasn't amazed and impressed and marveling was Uncle Bud's mom, grandma Hett - she simply said "he WAS Bud's horse, you know, he just came to say "Good-by."" I guess it's true, truth is sometimes stranger than fiction - it really doesn't have to make sense.

But that hasn't kept me from playing that picture over and over in my mind over the past 30 years, the horses running, the skies clearing and somewhere out there, perhaps, Uncle Bud, laughing at my amazement.

Antiquity

While prowling through the antique stores yesterday, I realized that half of the furniture was from the 1950's. I was astounded! 1950's, golly, that's just - it's just - 45!! Years ago? The realization of what exactly that meant set my ample fanny immediately down on the closest chair - a chrome legged, yellow vinyl topped number (reminiscent of the one in OUR kitchen in Rapid City, South Dakota a few years back - actually, let's see, maybe more than a "few" - maybe 45 years ago).

The many colored "tinnish" glasses brought back memories of tall cool glasses of "Kool Aid" -(the rivulets of condensation always ran down the sides of the glass, down our arms and off the elbow) and a bunch of the "kids" standing in our kitchen. Bikes were normally thrown indiscriminately against the front fence and various pet dogs waited for the return to the streets with Master or Mistress.

My mom, known as "Katrie" to my friends, always had freshly baked cookies stashed in one of those big, polished, tin containers with the black knob on top. (I saw one yesterday!) She was a whiz in the kitchen and could whip up a batch of ham salad sandwiches in about 15 seconds - we'd gobble, we'd drink, we'd grab a handful of chocolate chip cookies and away we'd go.

Life was good in Rapid City, South Dakota, in the late 40's and 50's for the Riegers. My dad, known to the kids as "Friegie" (behind his back only!) never had much time for us - he was always busy. Busy doing things that, I guess, Dads were SUPPOSE to do back then - hunting, fishing, building stuff, panning for gold (honest) and holding down his "real" job with the Government as a CAA Inspector. He wasn't, as my mom was, a kid lover - he tolerated us, within reason, but he didn't get involved.

The living room was the sanctuary for my dad - he sat in "his" chair - and woe is it to anyone who accidentally sat there - adult or child. He would stand newspaper in hand, staring at THE chair and sitter therein. Usually it meant a fast retreat for the interloper, and then Dad would settle in, with a sigh, and snap the paper out in front of him and begin the arduous task of cover to cover reading. I remember the furniture as though it were yesterday - dark blue, kind of a prickly velvet stuff - the arms were worn smooth, but mom had little white doilies hiding THAT fact. I would wait, impatiently, to talk to dad, legs being prickled by that darned prickly velvet stuff on the couch, until he was done, and chances of a positive answer were much better.

We, of course, during that time were a "one-car" family, as were most folks we knew, and walking to the movies, in the evening, for mom and me was as normal as apple pie. When dad traded in our 1940 Olds for a 1954 Olds with air conditioning! It was life in the fast lane for the Riegers. Wonders continued, as a couple of years later, dad appeared with a Jeep pickup and we became a "two-car" family. The Jeep eventually became mine and I promptly drove it to the top of "M" Hill on my first outing and couldn't get it down - it was too steep to turn around and to high to continue. Dad was not as impressed as my friends were as he drove it back down, and I lost my Jeep privileges almost as soon as I got them.

The Antique Stores took me on a tour of my own "Antiquity" yesterday, and it was as good as the memories it invoked.

The Moms

Ladies, whether you are one or want to be one or aren't one and don't want to be one, you still had one! Let's face it; there is a mom in all of our pasts. "moms", "mamas", "mothers" "mommies" - various and sundry sizes and shapes and dispositions and personalities, but moms, none the less.

I didn't realize it at first, (MY mom knew it, but didn't tell me) that you lost your given name when your children start School - it wasn't even gradual - my daughter, Tracy, entered grade school, bam! I was known as "Tracy's mom". Not, of course, to be confused with the four years, when she was in High School, playing basketball, and I became "25's Mother". (My mom said she was "Phyl's mom" for so long she forgot she had a name!)

At any rate, the years have passed and Tracy has become an adult - I remember, as a young adult, my relationship with my mom. The gradual transition from her guiding me into adulthood, to my guiding her in her senior years (she would kill me for saying "senior" years!). Helping with her business affairs as I grew strong in my own businesses and advising her, as I was learning, of good books and special programs and the like. Reminiscent of my youth, when she would drag me to the Doctor's office when I was sick, I began threatening her with just such visits if she wouldn't go to the doctor on her own for one ailment or another.

The "Rules of Mommiehood" had changed and the roles of mother and daughter became blurred and then reversed completely. And within our circle of friends, she went from being "Phyl's Mom", to me being "Kay's daughter".

My daughter and I had not had the luxury of spending those years doing our usual mom and daughter thing, as she lived in Athens, Greece. Even if my pocketbook could handle it, I doubt if my schedule could have handled frequent trips over to see her, but that year, we just threw caution to the wind and mom went to visit! My trip was a vacation in all aspects - we played Scrabble and read books and we shopped in the heart of the City. We visited the Parthenon and traveled the countryside. She played tour guide -ordering in Greek and instructing me not to get the --- or to be certain to try the ---. But it wasn't until we spent two days at a small island outside Athens that I realized what was happening!!

We arrived at the Isle of Spetses around noon - we had come over on the Hydrofoil; a horse drawn carriage took us from boat to hotel and we promptly readied ourselves for some type expedition - renting small motor scooters, we took to the hills. Truthfully, it wasn't until we were speeding up the road on our mopeds that I realized just what was going on. She was in front on her bike, I was dutifully putt-putting, on MY bike, some 100 yards behind... "Mom, watch for the loose gravel!" - "Can you understand the shifting?" As we stopped and started our trek down to the water, she went ahead and cautioned "Be careful here, mom, it's pretty steep - do you think you can make it back up this incline??" "Here, take my hand, let me help you!"

In the recess of my mind, I recalled a blond, pony-tailed youngster, wobbling ahead of me on a new bike. I could hear my own voice cautioning "Honey, please, don't go on the loose gravel." - "Tracy, please pull over to the side if a car comes" "Be careful, but don't worry, mom's here if you fall - I'll help you"

Then suddenly the mother becomes the mothered - the leader becomes the led, and the not so gradual transition of youth to age has begun and as someone once said "I've barely "Begun the Beguine" and it's "Good-Night Ladies" *already!*"

I think I'm going to like this!

Christmas in Virginia

I kept envisioning that T-shirt that says "Mirror, mirror on the wall, I've become my mother after all", as I stood hesitantly in the doorway to the outside. Heck, I am just "the mom" coming to visit - I'm no longer that impulsive, devil-may-care youth that I was last year. Consequently, there I stood in the doorway, scantily clad in one of Tracy's old swim suits, thinking, I feel certain, just about the same things that my mom would think were she here.

The snow on the deck was fresh, and even from inside the doorway, I could see my own breath in the crisp morning air. The dye was cast from the very beginning, and I knew that my refusal to participate would never be accepted. "Nooooo, Tracy, I really don't think that I can do this. I'll catch a cold, I just got over the flu, this is 'way different weather from the Valley - please, please don't make me do this!"

It seems unnatural the way she turns her head to Steve (could her head spin all the way around at any minute?) and they beckon to me "- come in Mom, come in. You'll love it - you'll really love it." Is it possible that I am suspicious of my own child, she wouldn't (would she?) lure me in to my possible injury, or would she?

It was with a certain amount of fear and trepidation that I crunch across the crisp snow and plunk my ample bottom onto the side, only to notice that the steam has turned to ice on the edge of the deck! I momentarily worry that, perhaps, like in those days of yore, when I was challenged to stick my warm tongue onto the freezing pipe, it couldn't be removed! I actually grin to myself at this prospect, wondering what the fire department will say when then arrive to torch some middle aged lady's rear off the side of the deck.

So far, so good, with the tentative touching down of the first foot into the steaming water. Slowly now, dropping the towel onto the snow covered deck, and nervously clutching the sides, I lower myself into the bubbling hot tub. (Steve, who said, during the negotiation stage of my hot tub/snow mass experience, that he would close his eyes for my towel dropping entrance into the tub, discretely stares into the depths of the pool..) In retrospect, I believe that this was for his own well being as much as for my personal comfort. He probably would have had to laugh, and I would have had to hurt him.

From my particular vantage point in the "best seat" in the tub (the one with the moving back massager) I loll back and stare up into the tall, but Winter-barren trees that surround the house and deck. Large crows glide onto the branches above us, and the gray squirrels scamper from bird feeder to bird feeder. A few of the braver Cardinals sit at one of the feeders, and suddenly it all felt just right to me.

Perhaps I should have had more faith in these kids of mine - life was good there in the old hot tub. Three loved ones attired in three Santa hats on a frigid Christmas morning in Virginia; it doesn't get a whole lot better than that. Even the sprint from tub to house (barefoot in the snow) didn't diminish my enthusiasm. I felt fairly brave and adventuresome and laughed as I removed the tiny ice cycles from the hair at the back of my neck.

Then I sneezed.

The Forever Mom

Actually, I sat in much the same spot where I sat 25 years ago; eyes scanning the waves for the bobbing blond head of my daughter– who rode the waves and screamed "watch this, mom, watch this!" Stomach clenching and heart pounding, I watched her become her own person out there in the waves. Her eyes very seldom left the shore, where I loitered, acting like I really wasn't paying that much attention. I applauded her dazzling feats, and sweat the sweat of the mom who couldn't swim, but would possibly walk out on the water had I seen her flounder. She and Jamie (her best friend) played the game Marco Polo, and I wondered where I would buy earplugs before the games were through.

She was a little girl then, long legs with slightly knobby knees (much to her dismay) and a long golden ponytail. She was brown as a berry from top of head to bottom of feet. She labored over her tan, even then, and my own mom scolded her about her nose falling off from cancer (we lumped that in with the "if you run with a stick you will poke your eye out" remark). She was such a joy to me, and my friends always asked me "So! How's Tracy? Still perfect?" I would blushingly lower my eyes and admit– "Yes, she is."

Now, 25 years later, I am sitting on the beach, ample fanny placed on a "boogie board", with hands behind me, holding me in a position that I can see my only child, once again, ride the waves. I was out there with her for just a few moments, but in my cowardliness and fear of the water, I tried to entice her back to shore with me almost immediately. "No, mom, you go ahead, I will stay in for a few moments longer." I tried to look beseechingly at her and even made the mistake of saying– "You just come on back to shore, young lady, there is a terrible undertow out here!" She laughed and plunged in deeper and hit one of the bigger waves! I ran like the devil to the shore, where I took my place among other parents watching their children.

Then, I noticed that the parents watching *their* children from the shore, were approximately the same age as MY child out there in that big dangerous ocean. Wait a darn minute here.....

Closing my eyes, I remember my mom calling me her "kid" until the day she died. She nagged me about driving barefooted, and spending too much time by the pool– she said she worried... I laughed at her then– not realizing that the mom thing goes on forever.

My Tracy lives in the City now, and while she would love to be a golden goddess, she is pale and un-suntanned. She wants to return back up North with a golden tan but with a four-day window for tanning, we are beginning to wonder. I watch her roll in from the beach now, no longer with knobby knees, but with unflinching confidence and a grin I can see (even with my feeble old eyes) from my vantage point here with the other "parents".

You may think I exaggerate when I say the "mom thing"– but ever notice when you are at market and a little kid cries out "MOM!" A dozen heads jerk around to look– a dozen moms, perhaps, just like me who forget their little kids are no longer little kids.

It's a great thing, this Mom thing...

Journeys

The many journeys that we have taken over these years come back to tease me with thoughts of Bedouin tents nestling in the desert sands; the Bedouin soldier with the vivid scar across his face and the tattooed tears coming down from his wife's eye. I see them now, in the memories of my mind, as they sit across from me in the station.

The camels driven across the desert, on leg tied up to keep them from running away, and the great and gentle camel that I rode to see the Sphinx – bring back the burning sun and the courageous animals indentured there to keep the tourists happy.

Ireland – the magnificent Ireland – forever in my dreams!

Ireland- The Journey

As we are crossing the Ocean to go to Ireland, flashes of songs from my youth spring into my mind: Galway Bay, McNamara's Band, My Wild Irish Rose, gosh, and so many others. I sing away under my breath and feel as though I know where I am going, although, in retrospect, I had no idea.

We fly in over the patchwork quilt that is Ireland early of a morning and the beauty that spreads out below us takes our breath away. Greens in every shade and texture boggle the mind and the "patchwork" of the fields is so very real because the fences are hedges and stone, turning the land to three-dimensional. My pal, Kathleen, and I, with noses pressed to the airplane window comment on the clouds, which, as nearly as I can tell, are long gentle fog lines interspersed between the hilly regions.

Our accommodations left nothing to the imagination, glorious old manors with hand carved doors and wood paneling. The view from our room kept us standing like statues, for directly beneath our window was a wide, rapidly flowing stream, and behind that a "flowing" golf course. It appeared to spread across the greens and sand traps as though it were painted upon canvas. Had we not seen the golfers in their plaid pants and gaily-colored shirts I would have rubbed my eyes to make certain I was seeing something real.

Khristiene, our beautiful guide, told us stories while the bus drove through the winding roads, and we sat like children on the edges of our seats awaiting her next words. She told us of a country where 56 percent of the population owned their own homes, she told us of a country that had almost 100 percent graduation rate from high school and a phenomenal rate of college graduates. So many Irish students graduated from college, that there was a terrific brain drain with students leaving for other countries for jobs. The job market there was brim full as she put it, and they prayed for new high tech companies to come so their students would come home.

I, of course, watched the animals and was shocked to see that most of the cows, horses and sheep were lying down during our morning excursions. Apparently the feed is so lush that they eat their fill, and spend the rest their time lolling in the deep grasses.

We sang in the pubs while Kathleen's Aunt Pat did an Irish jig and I idly wondered to myself what sort of tourists we would had been had we all drank. We were wild and wooly enough with one dark glass of Guinness. When we toured the Jamison Whiskey Plant, Kathleen's Aunt Sue became one of the "testers". She rose to the occasion and polished off 6 little shots of Jameson's whiskey. While she suffered no ill effects, the bus people certainly eyed her with new respect!

What started out as a long trip to a strange place turned out to be a long trip to a place that knew no strangers. Our busload of "strangers" was now a busload of friends– "Top of the mornin' to ya!" "And the rest of the day to you!" we called out as we left– and I can tell you as a fact– Irish eyes are indeed smiling!

Land Of Contrast

When Tracy lived in Amman, Jordan a few years ago, and I went to visit, who would have known I would fall in love with a country?

The first step toward a "side trip" from Amman is hiring a "service" (pronounced ser-vees) which means a driver and a 25-year-old auto. Damascus is a 3-hour drive with exit and entry points in between. It is easier to have a driver as they help get you through all of the paperwork and miscellaneous stuff as you exit the Jordanian border and enter Syria. Mohammed is "our" man and he does well - using Tracy's Diplomatic Passport to its best advantage. We pass large groups of travelers with many bags and I don't even *want* to know if currency is changing hands. The diplomatic passport is respected in the Mid-East Countries far more than in the European nations. Tracy said she really didn't know why, other than we, as a Nation, have been extremely good to the Mid-East. For the most part, I believe that everyone we met was American friendly. Phew.

We arrive at the Jordanian exit point very early (6:30 am and they are just "cleaning up" - a "janitor" is whipping back and forth splashing water from a coffee can on to the floor— or, in our case, onto our pant legs and into our shoes.) We get through it, but with lots of giggles and wet feet. Back in the Cab, we careen on toward the next point of entry. Between these two countries is a "no man's" land where the sides of the road are littered with burned out cars (possibly bombed out??) and we speculate on who, what and why?

At the Syrian Border, they insist that (after the red tape and checking of Passport and Visas) we leave $100 American money for "safekeeping" and in return they give us Syrian pounds in exchange. Enterprising, I thought. Tracy tells me that, when we return back through this point on the way home, they will give us $98– minus purchases - in American back for our receipt.

When we arrive in Damascus the driver must remain (with a hundred or so other drivers and their cars) in a compound that is guarded by soldiers. We flag a local cab, and are off to the Souk (the Mid East equivalent to the Market in Mexico). There are several downtown acres of shop after shop. The streets are teeming with people, touting their wares and beckoning to us to come on in. Several recognize Tracy and call out enthusiastically - she is an obvious good customer - and we wade on in to the stores!

When we finally gather Mohammed at the driver's compound, we are bearing many parcels - from a brass lunch box for Rodd to a leather horse for Sandy and painted gourd for Esau. Home, Mohammed, por favor! Home.

The following morning, Tracy was off to work - so I was left to my own wiles. Squiggs and I begin our jaunt around the neighborhood. I, by now, am attired in Arab long dress and sandals, and Squiggs looks particularly fetching in her Barbara Bush pearls. We walk, and I gawk at the homes and landscaping - it is a lovely area, and the locals greet me like an old friend.

Noontime is test time for me and I have to catch a cab (alone!!) to the Embassy - hey, no problem. Before long, I am doing the "street-crossing dance" - namely crossing mid street - no light. They do not honor stop signs or stop lights– It's a touch and go experience, the instructions are that you are to simply begin across and never look at the cars. It would take a stronger person than I, so consequently there is much leaping, pausing, and looking pathetic! Finally I stand before the Embassy door; wild eyed, hair askew, but unscathed.

After lunch I go to visit the "Save the Children" headquarters. They sell rugs made by Bedouin women. The rugs, of course, are hand loomed - on the ground outside their tents. This is a first for the Bedouin women as they have never been gainfully employed - but times are tough and the nomadic life is getting more difficult. They know that their children must eventually be educated and clothed. Save The Children has 700 women weaving rugs - the organization takes the clean wool to them and also the dyes. The Executive Director, Helena Sayegh, is a beautiful 26 year old woman (unmarried, much to her father's chagrin) born in Jordan, educated in the US, but is Palestinian. She said that her parents were wealthy when they lived in Palestine, but when they were ousted; they walked to Jordan with nothing but the clothing on their backs.

Tracy's boss hosted an office party that night at his home. The home itself was magnificent - all done in whites except for the heavy hand made carpets on the floors. Marble and tile abounds and the china closets are filled with local art and brass.

This is a home that is passed from Top Management to Top Management as transfers occur. The exact furnishings change slightly due to personal preference, but I was interested to hear that the servants "went with the house". I wondered of the tales they could tell from over the years of high level diplomatic parties and living.

Balconies circled the upper floors, and we stood, wine glasses in hand, visiting and gazing off into the clear Jordan evening. The blue lights that top the Mosques are visible everywhere and I felt as though I had entered into the World of Ali Baba. I fell in love with this land of contrasts– with this land of dawn chanting and Bedouin tents encircling the City. One day, perhaps, I will return to ride that Arab horse back up the road to Petra. Perhaps, perhaps only in my dreams.

Egypt- The Journey

Friday morning, our first day in Egypt, Tracy and I were anxious to hit the bricks, and with a driver and van with air-conditioning, we leapt into the fray. The traffic was unbelievable, and we darted through traffic with horn blaring. The trucks and the busses were side by side with the donkeys with their heads down, pulling carts with mammoth loads.

First stop, the camel market (which seemed like a good idea at the time). Tourists were the exception here, not the rule, and we launched off on foot. Camels, in bunches, were being driven in all directions. They are pitifully thin as they had been crossing the desert for as long as 30 days to reach this particular market. Each has one front leg tied up to keep them from escaping and I wondered of the pain they must suffer for so long a journey. I was glad I went, but would never return.

The "Mud Man" factory is next, it is just opening, and the workers are stoking up furnaces, and (honest) they are making mud in a corner. The little figures and vases with figures emerging are not only fascinating, but intricate and beautiful as well. We unwisely purchase two large vases and many small items— what were we thinking?

Of course, we are now too laden down to proceed shopping, and we go back to the hotel and have a Rio Grande Valley Burger at the restaurant. Small world, isn't it?

Saturday is to be Pyramid day so we spend a quiet evening at the hotel after venturing out to eat. One pyramid is so close you can see it from the hotel window and I stand on the balcony that evening, envisioning bearded men racing Arabian horses across the desert sands. Visions of white tents with lavish pillows littering floors fill my mind and I anxiously await the morning.

The trip to the furthest pyramids at Sakara was a taxi trip through winding, narrow and busy roads. Donkeys and horses compete for lanes with the honking truck and taxi drivers. We arrive at the Sphinx and the related pyramids by 10 AM, a trifle harried but undaunted and ready for adventure! It is everything you have dreamed of, the miles of sand and the stark reality of the pyramids rising from the desert floor.

Our guide wasn't exactly Lawrence of Arabia, but he was enthusiastic and friendly and away we went to explore the "digs" and the mummies and the treasures therein. It was unbelievable to see the artwork and decorations on the interior of the pyramids. The open tombs are empty, but for a 5-dinar piece extra, we get to see the "never before seen" (oh yeah) tomb below— we cheerfully pay up and troop down the path. There are three bodies; two still wrapped, and one with a bony leg protruding. We are sweating and hot, and the excitement of the moment, prompts our guide to suddenly fan us with his "skirts" to cool us down. Needless to say, we now have first hand knowledge of what they DO wear under their robes. To be honest with you, I believe that it was more than we wanted to know.

Coming up from down under, we are immediately approached by a camel driver, and we crawl aboard the "ship of the desert" and, along with a guide, fly through the soft sand on the grouchy, but smooth as silk camels. Whatever apprehension we had about the camels quickly dissipated and we rocked on through the land of yesterday where movies are made and, in this case, dreams came true.

The afternoon netted a trip to the Museum in Cairo and lo and behold, the entire King Tut collection! Much like children, we fingered the glass that held the golden treasures; the tiny solid gold shoes and the wafer thin gloves of gold. The earrings he wore, with the posts the size of pencils, gave us cause to study his ear lobes in the golden mask— yep, large, large holes! We pressed our faces against the huge glass boxes that held the multiple covers for the tomb— all solid gold, and we were filled with awe.

Life was good for the Griggs girls in this country of marvels, and we filed another set of memories into our mental treasure trove.

Old Friends

Seems as though the "old" friends are the friends of our youth; the young, enthusiastic friends who pass through our lives as we grow into maturity. Those memories and those friends stay permanently recorded in my storehouse of memories. My friends from my old home in Rapid City.

My *old* friends – who became a part of the tapestry of my life.

The Last of the Real Cowboys

Tracy's dad, Norm, and I had many friends there in Rapid City, South Dakota, though probably none so close as our friend, Pat Trucano. While we felt that we all were "cowboys", probably Pat was the only true cowboy among us. Not that we all didn't ride, move cattle and, occasionally, get bucked off on our rears, for we did. We did, however, eventually get cleaned up and go to "real" work the next day. Pat was always a cowboy– in real life and on the weekends as well, he just had a cowboy mind set.

Pat, actually, was born a couple of generations too late, I guess– he was a chap wearing, snuff chewing, sleep on the ground and eat beans kind of guy. No task was too formidable for Pat; he could improvise and economize by making stuff out of nothing. Should we need a feeder or a trough and indicate that to Pat, the next day he would come driving up– his dog, Spike, standing tall on the seat next to him, the rack on his pickup clattering, and various tools and tanks neatly lined up in the back. With very little fanfare, he would then weld together some cast off water heater or surplus pipe to make the item of our dreams.

He wasn't a big guy– probably 5'8"– but wiry and tough as rawhide. His horse, Prince, was as leggy and tall, as Pat was short and compact. The two made an unlikely pair as they set off to bring the calves in to brand or to rope up a steer. My friend, Jaynell and I teased him unmercifully about his horse being called Prince, and we unflattering called old Prince "Paw's Prints" which set Pat's lip to twitchin' something fierce.

He was a bachelor, not due to any lack of ladies looking in his direction, but rather a self imposed bachelorism; for Pat had become the surrogate "dad" to his two sisters when his own father died. After Mary and Joan married, Pat finally married into a ready made family, and I mourned that he hadn't had his own son to bring up as a cowboy.

Pat's ever present cowboy hat was what I referred to as a "three-way roller"– the sides correctly rolled in– the back rolled in because of the close proximity of the back window of the pickup– winter's hat was black felt, and, of course, for summer, straw. His work boots were thick soled and battered, his dress boots, quite another matter– polished to glistening mirrored finish, and only worn for special occasions. When he appeared at our place in his bib overalls and baseball hat, we were in for some type of project– welding, hammering, sawing or the like.

In this day and age, you would probably say that 'we hung out"– but back then, we were all simply friends. We worked hard, laughed a lot, and I never even realized that those days wove the fabric of memories that bring South Dakota back to me again and again.

Jaynell called me the same day, last week, that Norm did, to tell me that our friend, Pat, had suffered a stroke. It has been 35+- years ago that we worked so hard and laughed so hard– leaning against the corral fence with a beer, listening to Jim Reeves on the pickup radio. Probably never once during that 35 years have I ever thought of Pat in any way other than that 25-year-old cowboy sitting up tall on old "Prints".

Pat's going to be all right, they tell me. I suppose they see him, there in the hospital, as just another 60-year-old sick man, but I will forever know him as one of the last real cowboys.

Best Friends

We were best friends 'way back when in Rapid City, South Dakota. 'Way back when meaning 'waaaaaaay back when!!

Our friendship started in 8th grade - we were "horse lovers" as my Dad called us. We spent many an hour slumped under a tree with reins to our trusty mounts held loosely in our hands, and the saddle-less horses grazed contentedly. What amazing stories kept us so enthralled, I don't, at this writing, remember, but they were grand. We could, however, upon a moment's notice, spring to our feet and onto the backs of the horses, and race away, laughing and cooking up other tales to tell under the next tree some miles up the pasture.

As we got older, Sandy went off to College and I got married, and our lives changed forever. After College, she returned to the area where she and I still met and rode our horses and went to horse shows and rodeos. Then as we each divorced and remarried - we moved to opposite ends of the Country. She to northern South Dakota, and I, of course, came to McAllen.

My relationship with Sandy never changed although we moved from Rapid City. Through the years we "kept in touch" through our moms (who, of course, remained in Rapid City). After Sandy's mom, Rachael, died, Sandy was thrust into a series of personal tragedies that kept us on the phone many times a week for over the following years. Her husband of 16 years died suddenly of a heart attack and shortly thereafter her 19 year old son, Michael, was kidnapped and murdered.

So, in 1986, when we met, face to face, for the first time in fourteen years, it was rather like seeing our own Mothers deplane. We had gone from the far edge of youth into full-blown middle age. We both wanted to say "You haven't changed a bit!" but nothing could have been further from the truth. (I maintained I looked exactly the same! But she just snickered disrespectfully!)

The tragedy of the murder had, in fact, turned her hair prematurely gray and she was tortured with continuous nightmares during the infrequent times when she slept. But Sandy was Sandy and she, although sometimes bitter and always agonizing moved forward with her life and began on a regular basis to visit South Texas.

Eight years have passed since Michael died. Sandy's work counseling parents of murdered children in South Dakota and surrounding States seems to have helped her - she doesn't forgive or forget, but she helps others cope and go on.

Now, rather than sitting slumped under a tree, horses in tow, we sit in the lawn chairs (much like our moms probably did) or walk down the beach at Padre. We laugh and speak of the days in South Dakota wistfully - were we really that crazy - did we really ride THAT long? And we speak of our moms and speak softly of Michael and we speak of friends who have fallen by the wayside. We do visit, at length, about her remaining son, David, in Croatia, and her grandchildren waiting in England for him to come home. And we speak of my daughter Tracy and my love for her.

And we walk, and we talk, and our forty-plus years of friendship seems as new and as special as it did 'way back then, sitting under that tree.

Robin Hood

Parties were the usual, not the unusual, there in Rapid City, South Dakota, in the mid-sixties. We were all about the same age, husbands, wives, an occasional single (who, of course, was loved by all) and we all liked to party. Any occasion, any holiday, was sufficient cause for us to roll out the entertainment gear and start preparations for something so out of the ordinary, so unexpectedly bizarre, and so much fun that folks outside of our little gang of 15 or so couples looked on with amazement.

Heck, we just thought it was the norm– Nancy Dunham was our guru and she made up elaborate menus and detailed game plans. We did sing-a longs, and she had made up word sheets that were given to each of us– we chimed in with Rusty Warren and the Barroom Buddies (among other groups) and thought we were wonderful. We lived our lives as though each day was our last.

Of course, every guru has to have that pices de resistance, that one spectacular, that one annual event that draws enthusiasm for the entire 11 months preceding it. Halloween was that event. We planned and schemed for months, we gathered material from the library and read up on eras– we tackled the annual Halloween party with determination and single mindedness.

Alas, there were just a few who were clever enough to make up their own costume Nancy, of course, was one– she and George came as aliens one year with heads made out of lighted egg cartons– a masterpiece and we all writhed with envy.

Norm and I were already plotting our next costumes– he was to go as a sheik and I as a harem girl, and we ordered our costumes from the only costume shop in the State. Our friend, Don Johnson, a quiet, bespectacled young man, a few years our senior, was mournful that he was the only one who would be shown up at the annual Halloween Spectacular– no costume! A last minute, urgent call to the costume shop in Sioux Falls determined his fate– only one costume left in the shop– Robin Hood.

Now he wasn't as enthused as we all were, but he readied himself for the promised "costume" that arrived, along with my harem outfit and Norm's sheik outfit, in a box, a wrinkled, smelly, and tangled mess two days before Halloween.

The women, of course, had taken Don on as a personal project, and we got him over to the house and prepared him for the worst– which, as it turned out, was the case. Lo and behold, Robin of Sherwood's body stocking would have set his merry men a laughing for days– the costume consisted of a pair of long underwear– dyed green, a dark green felt sling-thing to (we guessed) carry his arrows and a jaunty (at one time, I'm certain) green cap of green felt. A little pair of green felt footsies (with perky turned up toes) completed the outfit.

He actually looked sillier than he felt, if possible, but we assured him that in the festivity of the party, he would be just fine. He was a good sport, and we got a long feather and placed it in his perky green felt hat and he *was* just fine. Of course, from that day 'til this, we all called him "Robin".

Many years after that wonderful, crazy party when Robin entered society in his dyed green underwear with the feather in his hat, Rapid City suffered a monstrous flood and Robin Hood was last seen, close to midnight, reaching over the edge of the bridge for children careening through the water on a tree limbs. He passed one child back, but when they returned for the next, he was gone. His car was left with driver door open, and he vanished into the night and the water. When his body was found, days later, we all talked of him and his costume and our party and we were proud that he was our Robin Hood– forever.

The Littlest Rancher

The recent loss of my friend Jaynell's mom has prompted many long distance calls between Rapid City, South Dakota, and South Texas. With Mother's Day just around the corner it just appeared that her mom was the last of the "old" moms of our generation.

Jaynell's mom had been courted and won, in 1923, by one of western South Dakota's "bad boys" - Maurice "Coots" Higgins. He was a gambling man; he liked to drink the hard stuff and sit in the local saloons with a cigar and a good poker hand. When a troop of touring dancers came from New York City, to Casper, Wyoming, he gazed, with wonder, upon the tiny lead dancer in the show. He promptly fell in love although; she was so dainty, so frail, and so totally inappropriate for ranch country and a gamblin'man. He was as handsome and dashing as any storybook scoundrel, and the only thing he loved more than a challenge was a beautiful woman - they were soon married and moved back to Coots' home in South Dakota.

Mom Higgins had been raised with the arts in New York City, and had even danced on Broadway! Her unique courage and sense of adventure led her to a touring dance group. This, of course, was during a time that Ladies didn't have the liberated spirit that they do now, and she was, obviously, a trendsetter! She was no bigger than a minute, and according to local historians, she was more beautiful than any woman who had ever stepped off of the train there in Scenic, South Dakota. Her long brown hair nearly reached her 18 inch waist, and her fashionable attire was regarded with unconcealed amazement. When Jaynell's mom came to South Dakota in the '20s, I'm certain that she had no idea what she had in store for her.

Her trunks, hat boxes and suitcases littered the baggage area and the assembled crowd stared with bewildered eyes. Did the Lady not know where they were? Did she not realize that this was cattle country where women had children as well as worked shoulder to shoulder with their husbands? There she stood, that tiny little stranger from New York, wearing a fine gray wool suit, matching hat and a treasured pair of gray kid leather gloves with a pearl button at the wrist. The neighbors vowed that she would never; never make it there in South Dakota.

Jaynell said that her mom never complained, that she moved to the ranch, with the path to the toilet, with the garden to plant and the water to haul and bent to her task of having children and working shoulder to shoulder with her husband.

The major problem at that point was that Coots wasn't all that interested in working - period. So Mom Higgins just raised her four daughters and worked and taught them to work as well.

Jaynell and her mom were my friends and neighbors there in Rapid Valley, but mom Higgins was as tough as Jaynell and I put together. She walked the corrals carrying a tall walking stick - and from any distance, it appeared the stick was walking on its own. She would be sauntering amidst the dairy cattle - poking this one and that to get them to move on, but her head wasn't as tall as their backs and her 90-pound frame hardly compared to "the big dry cow" (as we called her) who probably weighed in at 1200 pounds. She ran the dairy back then (30 years ago) with an iron hand and the 80 cows they milked kept them working from dawn 'til dusk.

She was then 66 years old, back when we were neighbors - thirty years ago. She could mow a field of alfalfa without breaking a sweat and still rode her horse, Major, to bring the cows in from the fields - even though she was nearly blind from cataracts. She moved into the nursing home when she was close to 90 - until that time, she still walked in the fields and questioned the condition of the cattle and the quality of the grass.

She died last month, this tiny lady from New York who "would never make it" on a South Dakota ranch. She was still a Lady, and although 74 years of baling hay and tending cattle had, perhaps, callused her hands and bent her back, they found, neatly folded, in the back of her trunk, among the remnants of a life long gone, a pair of gray kid gloves, with a single pearl button at the wrist.

The Perfect Shell

Christmas wasn't a favorite time during those early years for my friend Sandy and me. Her son was in England, then Croatia and my daughter was living in Jordan and then Athens. Sandy spent lonely Christmases in South Dakota, and I, alone, here. We usually spent the holidays mulling over better times, and happier Christmases via the telephone. When circumstances were just right, however, she came to the Valley, bag and baggage for the holidays.

We discovered that the Island was the perfect place for a couple of little old ladies such as us. That year that we found we could drive up the beach for 21 bouncy, breathtaking miles. We devoted our festivities to driving several miles, and then taking to the sand, walking the beach, seeking what we would call "the *perfect* shell". The perfect shell changed from day to day, and early of a morning, clad in several pair of warm-ups, hats, gloves and determination, we, with a single, shared vision of the perfect shell, walked for mile after mile.

When she moved to the Valley a few years ago, we maintained our, then, week-end vigil, more discriminating than before, but lugging home bags and boxes of the almost *perfect* shell - a glistening pink conch or a spiral staircase with pinks and lavenders ever circling. The sand dollars; bigger now, and yet sometimes as small as the nail on my littlest finger.

Slick could hardly wait for our dawn excursion to the beach - he had been huffing and puffing for several pre-dawn hours - wondering if it was time yet. Going from bed to bed, great nose gently nudging, softly inquiring - "Isn't it time YET??" It would still be dark when we would start piling on the warm ups, a quick drive to Rovan's netted coffee and sweet rolls - a Tupperware dish of fresh water in back for Slick and the journey begins - the search for the *perfect* shell.

That was a few years ago, those happy excursions to the Island. My friend had a heart attack the first year after she moved here; we did make a few runs to the Island after that, but early this year a near fatal accident left her hospitalized, then on crutches, then a cane for six months. As she recovered some of her mobility, she noted a small lump on her foot, and it was diagnosed as cancer three months ago.

Slick and I still go to the beach and still walk those long, windy beaches in the early hours of the morning. The last time we were there, I believe that I might just have found the *perfect* shell that we sought for so many Christmases. It was a beauty, a conch, about 10 inches long, with a pearlized interior of shades of pink and ivory. I knew at that moment, that moment that should have been perfect joy at finding the perfect shell, that Sandy's and my journey down the beach over those many years **WAS** the perfect shell. It wasn't what we sought, but what we found on every mile, the friendship, the sharing, and the love of the beach. I now see that we had found the perfect shell by just being there.

Sandy will come back to the Island with me soon. We probably won't be as relentless in our search, we will probably spend more time driving than walking, but, we will, in all probability, continue to seek the *perfect* shell.

New Year's Cowlamity

My most memorable New Year's Eve, was, of course, there in Rapid City, SD. Winter winds blew fiercely, snow getting heavier by the minute, the icy roads gleamed in the lights of the pickup truck, but it didn't matter to us... We were going to a dance - and like the mailmen of yore, neither snow nor sleet nor dead of night would stay us from our path to the Elks Club, there in Rapid Valley.

The dress I was wearing that evening was a glorious royal blue velvet, softly fitted, with ostrich feathers (blue also) at the hem. We whirled and waltzed to (our favorite) *The Blue Skirt Waltz* and an impressive display of tiny blue feathers fell to the floor and swirled about our flying feet.. I remember wondering if I would have a feather left if we danced one more. It was a wonderful night and we danced too much and drank too much.

As midnight approached, Norm decided that we should run home to check out the heifer that we thought was going to calf that night.

We drove directly to the corral - with the pickup lights shining on the fence, we could see her- she was down, straining, and in obvious trouble. The dash to the house was the finale for my remaining ostrich feathers -- they were brilliant there in the snow on the way in, and a ready trail on the way out. A quick change from dance attire to our usual boots, hats, jackets and gloves set us trudging back through the snow; wind now blowing with blinding force, on in to the corral.

This particular heifer was part Charlois - and part Brahma - and neither part was what you would call friendly. Norm calmly surveyed the situation and said - "Look, Phyl, I'll rope her and you run in front of her; she'll chase you around the post and she'll be easier to snub up." Sounded pretty good to me until I was in front of her - she was in pain, cold, hostile and doing a pretty good job of striking the ground with her front hoof, sending a shower of snow and corral dirt over her back. But a dancing girl such as I was (with a tiny bit too much of the bubbly) did the fancy footwork and led the old girl on a merry chase around the post... Snubbed up, with Norm doing the calf pulling, she was far more hostile when the calf was finally born than when I first circled the post with her on my heels. A fresh problem arose - how to *unsnub* her - by this time I was far less enthusiastic than before, when I had strains of *The Blue Skirt Waltz* ringing in my ears -so I declined the running and "unsnubbing" much to Norm's consternation.

We were close to frozen clear through by now; boots, goulashes and down filled jackets can only tide a person over for so long. It was nearing 3 am, snowing heavily, a wet, groggy, calf at our feet, and a wild, white cow, attached to a pole in the middle of the corral, just aching to get out of her confinement and hurt someone.

With much rope jiggling and coaxing, the rope began its unwinding from the post and I headed for one gate and Norm, tardily, headed for the other, just as she wrenched free. It wasn't a pretty sight, (actually, I guess *I* thought it was at the time) she came flying at him and just as he got to the fence, she gracefully put her head under his butt and threw him up and over like a bale of hay! He grabbed on to a rail on the way over and ended up just about standing on his head there in the snow - boots above the fence, cowboy hat and head right in the ground.

Obviously our New Year's Eve wasn't just exactly what we had planned, but it did brighten the beginning of our New Year, as you can imagine, and what a tale it was to tell at the next dance at the Elks Lodge.

Events

The events that shape our lives – for good or for bad; the happiness and the fearfulness, the giddy and the grave – perhaps temper us for all of the happenings we face.

The events that caused me to question my own persona – was I really so shallow that I would wait in the 100 degree sun for a hand shake? Would I really stand so devil may care there in the Oval Office?? Apparently so.

My lot was a lucky one as I wended by way through the truly bizarre and the stunningly horrible. I cam through unscathed and untouched as the World collapsed around us on September 11 – unscathed, but with a knowledge that it could happen to us!

The President Present

A month ago I really wasn't all that enthused that we were having the President of the United States down to McAllen. It was a "What?" "The President?" "Why?" When it was carefully explained to me by at least 50 people, the benefits and the honor and the "getting put on the map" of it. I did my "yeh, yeh" thing - but became a lot more impressed when I found out he was going to *our* Alonzo Cantu's house. Hmmmm. This was getting serious - sure, I remember being excited when Rush Limbaugh came to McAllen - and I remember standing in line to get Tony Dorsett's autograph. But the President of the United States? Hmmmmm...

A week ago, I was getting pretty enthused that we were having the President of the United States down to McAllen. It was a "When?" "Where?" How?" thing with me, and yesterday, it was a "Wow!" thing and today found me standing in the back yard of Alonzo's fabulous home with Republicans and Democrats, Hispanics and Anglos, friends and enemies, men, women and children (with a sharp shooter or two on the roof) all honoring, not only the President, but one of our own, Congressman Ruben Hinojosa.

Those of us who went early benefited by visiting with the myriad of folks there that we knew, but don't see all that often. We hashed and rehashed City, County and State business. We offered options on critical problems occurring throughout the nation, and we just plain visited and enjoyed a great morning.

Tina Martin and I stood together in a small grassy area to the right of where the President stood - we whispered repeatedly about the folks who pressed against the "rope line" (where he would eventually, after speaking, go and shake hands and allow pictures). We commented that we were amazed by the tenacity of those in the front, the commitment they had to stay in that particular spot for lo those many hours - just to shake his hand. We were horrified to see so many familiar faces up there - we, of course, would "love to have a picture taken", but something more **personal** - something just of us and the President - not any crowd scene. We were very righteous in our opinions - us, grovel? Us shove and crowd? Oh please!

Feet were weary and faces sunburned by the time Alonzo welcomed us to his home and introduced Congressman Hinojosa. Ruben wove a story for a spellbound audience (that included President Clinton) about the kindness that the President had shown during his appearance at the Tom Landry Stadium in Mission. The handicapped child that couldn't quite reach the fence, so the President could shake his hand. The President said "No problem!" and climbed up the fence to reach out to him. The other small child in a wheelchair, with tiny hands folded in his lap - unable to reach out- and the President placed his own left hand beneath the child's hands and enfolded them with his other.

It should have been a tough audience, all of those politicians, all of those professional goers-to-political functions folks, but there were also quite a few hands hastily wiping away tears after Ruben told us his story. The President blinked away a few tears himself before it was all over, and he, himself, warmed all of us standing there in the Rio Grande Valley sunshine. He spoke of children and education and tax incentives and people working together with other people, he spoke of all of those things that regularly happen here in McAllen. Respect for each other and common goals and hands across boundaries. He told us what we like to hear and he told us he was proud to be here and, quite frankly we were very, very proud that he was here too.

Tina and I watched as he proceeded toward the rope line and the waving arms and calls of "Mr. President - over here." Then, finally, as he turned toward us, we waved tentatively to encourage him to our grassy area, but it was a no go as he began his walk down into another area -down another rope line. Tina's and my eyes met for one fraction of a second, and with very little fanfare, and no hesitation whatsoever, we plunged into the fray. Hey, a little shoving and elbowing never hurt anyone, did it? We got our handshake and some of that great Clinton eye contact, and hastened off, laughing and feeling good. Our President came to McAllen and we were there!

The Chiefs And Me

My involvement was a spur of the moment thing– when the City Secretary called and asked if I would accompany our Chief of Police to a function in Washington, D.C. She said that the Mayor had requested that I go in his place– it left no guesswork on my part– ok, I'll go. When? Tomorrow– to return the next day - wow, you've got to be kidding!

Thursday, found me standing in line, with my single dress carry-on, at the airport with Chief Longoria. Chief told me that the trip was to formally receive a $2,256,000 grant from the Attorney General's office through the Organization C.O.P.S. (Community Oriented Policing Services). Armed with the instructions, the cab money and the hotel information– we were off to seek our fortunes in D.C.

We arrived in Baltimore after 9:30 PM, and the 45-minute drive from Baltimore to D.C. was livened up by our cab driver who sped through the streets of south Washington, slowing only to issue a challenge to another driver who pulled up beside us. I don't think that Chief was up to the chase, nor was I, but fear is a tremendous motivator, and we remained discretely silent as the cars raced side by side down the quiet streets.

The lobby of the hotel, early the next morning, teemed with other chiefs, uniformed and distinguished looking, and other (obviously) elected officials. By 9:30 we were marching from the Executive Office Building into the White House— 18 Chiefs and an equal number of mayors and other elected officials.

By this point, we were all pretty certain that something good was about to happen, but we weren't all that certain just what. We remained fixed on our course, and through the White House we went, studying portraits and sneaking looks in through half closed doors. (A bunch of maybe not-so-typical tourists, but doing a pretty credible job of imitating them.) We waited in the Roosevelt Conference Room, and visited like old friends. I was huddled with the Mayor of San Bernardino and the Mayor of Miami when the door flew open and Attorney General Janet Reno walked into the room

The men leapt to their feet and the ladies looked, with admiration, at the "first" power lady of the nation. I wish I could tell you that we all acted with decorum, but there was a rush to camera by the lot, and as she strode, smiling, down our ranks we did the best we could to look attentive, and not notice if our counterpart was, indeed, snapping that lens. She was gracious and had us raptly attentive as she asked questions about our communities. She thanked the Chiefs for the jobs they were doing back home, and asked what else she could do for us.

This "warm up" chat was merely a preview of things to come, and the door opened and a voice called out that the President was waiting for us in the Oval Office. It was a near stampede with Janet Reno leading the pack, the Chiefs following as a close second. As the elected official filed in behind, it was one of those moments you will cherish for a lifetime. The President waited at the door, shaking hands. He visited briefly with each of us. (I told him I was from the All America City of McAllen, and that he had been down to visit not too long ago— he gazed off briefly and said, "Yes, I remember. It was an informative trip!" We passed down the line, which included V.P. Al Gore, and Janet Reno and then out the door to the Rose Garden where the presentation would be made.

The program was long, and it was hot enough to fry an egg on any forehead (including the President's) but as we sat there in the steaming sun (I was wedged between two extremely ample Mayors from the East Coast) we were as happy as kids.

With the presentation over, Chief ambled off across the driveways, coat over his arm, and I walked along behind him. I was thinking because of this Chief of ours, the citizens of McAllen were safer by 28 officers; because of him, our City coffers were fuller by enough money to fund a crime prevention program. Because of his initiative and his love for this City, he, one person, had made all of this happen, and because of him, I had just waded through the insignia rug in the Oval Office. Whatta guy...

As suddenly as it had begun, it was over. We stood out on the street in front of the White House– just the two of us, two good old boys from South Texas, and we simply stared at each other. We were sweating and rumpled, and my feet were killing me. I guess it hit us at the same time; we started laughing and gave each other a high five, and walked away from our day in the sun. Whatta day.

The Day the Planes Came

We just didn't get it. We all pretty much stood there— staring up where we envisioned the loud speaker voice that had spoken to us. Quiet, no complaining, no joking, quiet. The loud speaker continued "If you live in Dallas— go home.

If you are going elsewhere— go home."

I stood, dumfounded, thinking only of myself, of course. How do I get home? Where do I stay? All of the things we are accustomed to think— me, me, me.

But, let me begin at the beginning, in Washington, DC, where, at 5:30 AM Tracy left me at the Dulles Airport to be whisked away home to McAllen— "I'll be home by 11!" I told her. "Great flight."

At approximately 8:30 AM our flight arrived at DFW. I rode the tram to Terminal B, while a lady visited with me about "a private plane had crashed into the World Trade Center", then, walking through the terminal I could see, in front of every small eating establishment, perhaps, 40 to 50 passengers standing neatly, line after line. Men with briefcases, women with rolling suitcases, every size and description of person— ladies in the saris and men with turbans, girls in shorts and boys in warm-ups. United they stood there, silent, eyes fastened to the television perched behind the counter. I noticed that the men, for the most part, had their arms folded across their chests, and the women held their purses to them.

Something bad had happened and we just didn't get it.

There at our gate, Gate B3, we waited impatiently to board. When an attendant told one passenger that the flight had been cancelled, a combined groan waved over us. Then the overhead speakers toned out in a ladies businesslike voice, "ALL flights have been cancelled– ALL airport facilities in America will cancel all flights and ALL airport facilities in the United States will be closed until further notice. If you are from Dallas or surrounding area, go home. If there is any way you can get home, go home."

Not a familiar face there in the lounge of B3, but I spotted a man who just looked like he knew what he was doing– I called out to him "Sir– sir, are you heading to McAllen?" He said, yes, he was, and I said "Let's get out of here and rent a car and drive down." He looked a bit taken aback to be picked up there in the lounge of Gate B3, but said– "let's do it".

During the hour wait for luggage, people milled from luggage carousel to luggage carousel uncomplaining and quiet. Cell phones are pressed to almost every ear– "yes, we are safe, yes, we are coming home." While some people just picked up their luggage, we picked up the third member of our "drive home" team, Betty Burt from Alamo. Another stranger, another strand to weave into our quilt of memories of September 11, 2001.

The bus ride to the rental car agencies was nearly silent, people sat, deep in their own thoughts; two ladies across from me spoke quietly to each other in German, tears running down their cheeks. The man sitting next to them had his head in his hands, but looked up to share with us that his brother-in-law was on the 100th floor of tower two. His sister had headed down there when she heard about the first crash, and got there in time to see the second plane crash into the other tower.

We arrive at the rental agencies to note that the interior of all of the Hertz, Avis, etc., rentals were overflowing with people and baggage. My new friend, Bob, ignored the lines and went to a manager, showing him his 5-star rating and the next thing I know we are circling away from DFW in a new Mercury Marquis, three strangers heading home. Three strangers linked forever because of a barbarian act that terrorized a nation.

We are well educated on the tragedies by the time we get home, radio picking up every moment of the days events as we hurtle down the highway. And, as the members of the Congress and the Senate stand on the steps of the Congress, singing "God Bless America" we place our hands on our hearts and sing along with them– tears running down our cheeks.

Something bad happened and a World is affected. God, please bless America and God bless us every one.

Valley Friends

And the pages fill to the praises and causes of my Valley Friends. My peers, my silly, serious and decent peers; they have arrived in droves to my "friend yard". They come bringing stories and friendship – a mature friendship now, a warmth, a closeness that we all crave, and seldom find.

My Valley friends – you have saved me here in my Valley home, you have loved me and comforted me. I thank you.

I Miss My Friend

It's been years now since I've seen my friend, and only at a distance at that. While it was a "falling out" as we are wont to say when things go awry with our friends, it was, at the time, a falling out with some sort of peace for me. In retrospect, it was during a time in my life when the problems seemed to pile higher and higher each day and I couldn't seem to let her know. Although she was my best friend, and although I was *her* best friend, she didn't even guess.

We, apparently, could no longer read each other thoughts. We were simply lost in our own particular reverie. Thus, the dearest and best friendship of my life was lost in some peculiar and curious (as though I stood apart and could see it happening) stage play. It was a peculiar thing between us, perhaps the culmination of many such peculiar things. Rather like the two ships at sea that withstood the fieriest storms, but, as it says, went down "when all was tranquility". We had certainly faced the storms, my friend and I, and we had stood side by side and laughed into the ensuing gale! We were steadfast in our search for the truth and all of the silliness that we could make of it! She in her Mickey Mouse ears and me in my polka dot bow tie.

The love of true friends is far reaching, and while occasionally threatened, normally never wavers. Yet, suddenly, amidst the falling of failed businesses and lawsuits and marriage, it was all over; just-another casualty in the never -ending pursuit of life.

Our worlds have many influences however, and in my dream last night I dreamed we were back on a field trip, my friend, my daughter and I. A trip from Atlantic City to Washington, DC, a trip we made during the Gulf War crisis. American flags flew daily throughout our country then and we alternately cried and saluted as we drove the back-way through small town after small town. Our destination was downtown Washington DC and we, quite by chance, encountered a group of Vietnam vets. They were circling on their Harleys– American Flags proudly flying from holders behind their bike seats! We solemnly stood with our hands on our hearts as they passed by.

Later, we sat on the steps of the Lincoln Monument and stared across the reflecting pond, and pondered the fate of our wonderful country, America. It was a glorious day for us and we sat, arm in arm, silently, thanking God for our country, our capital and our friendship.

I miss my friend.

The Ferryboat Ride

Curiosity drove with my friend Jacque and me to the Island this past weekend. We wondered how the bridge "looked" and how deserted the Island was and were the shells actually waist high as I predicted. We were curious as well as to the mechanics of the ferryboat that was to take **us**, and obviously this was a curiosity to every other Island lover as well.

The "staging" area at Port Isabel was lined with cars and trucks as we pulled in, and the orange-vested young man who directed us was cheerful and told us that we had, perhaps, as long as a 2 hour wait. It didn't detour us for a moment! We leaned our seats back and visited and, then, as the minutes became an hour, we wandered up and down the lines of cars, visiting, now, with other Island seekers. My big dog, Bob, trotted at my side, but as we got closer and closer to "go" we got back in the Bob Mobile and waited like the rest. I was amazed to see several men go forward to do the arm-waving / complaining about others who had gotten ahead of them and what were the orange-vested directors of traffic going to do about it.

It made me laugh out loud to think how unimportant his complaints were in the whole scheme of things, for from our vantage point we could see men working late into the night on the damaged causeway. I wondered how important it would be to those folks who made their living there at the Island that it took two or three people 20 minutes longer to arrive.

Driving down Padre Boulevard at 10 PM that evening, it was virtually a ghost town. An occasional car drove by and marked Police Cars carefully guided the guests who had waited patiently (and impatiently) to come over on the ferry down onto the "main drag".

Saturday morning, however, the Island was the Island. The streets were quiet, but clean, and many of the cyclists who had been moved to Harlingen for their Annual Outing (from the Island) were there in hoards. They, like the rest of us love the Island, and I will tell you that the Island loves them as well. Hotel and motel prices were rock bottom, and the Blue Marlin Grocery Store was stocked full. Yes, some stores were closed and others were doing abbreviated hours, but the locals that my pal, Jacque and I spoke with were happy to see the amount of folks that were there.

We drove the distance to the "6 Exit" where the ocean rolled and spray was flying. The water was cold, but not cold enough to keep us from wading out, into knee high waters, with sandals gripped firmly in hand. When you haven't been on the beach for a while, it just takes your breath away, and I regretted not having neglected my beach walking job for so long.

For Winter Visitors and folks who have some time to spare, a trip down is very worth while. The ferry is free and as you cross the waters from the mainland to the Island, the Dolphins frolic in your wake, and you know you are heading for a great adventure. Sixteen cars (and/or pickups) go on each small ferry and the large ferry can accommodate 45 cars or the trailer and truck equivalent. I know you can go by passenger boat if you don't want to take your car, and that is a marvelous adventure in itself.

South Padre Island needs us to come and visit; to walk the beaches and to shop the shops and eat in their restaurants. Have an adventure– it's the same old Island that we all know and love– it just takes a bit longer to get there! The waist high shells? Well, maybe next time!

The Simpson Place

The Simpson's are gone now. I stand on my usual perch, atop the diving board in my back yard, gazing toward their property, empty now, except for the fireplace standing, alone, where their living room was once. I remember the living room fondly, as it was a cheery place with red and white check upholstered furniture which encircled that very same fireplace. There was a mantle then with pictures of family and pictures of dogs in Santa hats sitting securely upon it.

I can tell you that my favorite place was at the huge dining room table (which, I always surmised, was crafted from timbers from some remote shed) with the family all sitting around criticizing Billy's barbecue spattered apron, or raving about Ginger's famous peach ice cream. I was a part of the family then, usually sitting next to Billy's Mom, Audrey (although I always called her MRS. Simpson) being entertained by her analysis of the World and City events. Ever marveling at her quick wit and keen mind (gosh, I don't even know how old she was then, but she was on top of everything!) Fred, Billy's dad, kept his end of the table entertained by spinning tales of Billy and the "boys" in their youth.

Ginger and I were particularly close, not only because our mutual love of the many birds and beasts that were contained between our two properties, but our tender hearts toward all living things. The slightest "event" would cause a hurried call to the other– an injured bird, an abused dog– we were sickening in our "it was the cutest thing" calls. Always regarding one of our animals, always reinforcing our love for them.

Billy was a giant among men for me as a neighbor. When the dogs attacked my goats, in the middle of the night, he scaled the barbwire fence between our properties in his night shorts, carrying a shotgun (although I wonder even now if he would have used it). And the night that Slick died, Billy and Ginger raced to the house at my call; Ginger and I clung to each other and wept, while Billy tenderly gathered Slick's body in a blanket, allowing his silken face to rest gently against his shoulder. He buried him beneath the mesquite tree in my yard early the next morning before I came home from work and marked the grave with a simple cross.

During this time of them moving up North, we have mourned the loss of the habitat for the Blue Herons and Ginger's Purple Martins have circled endlessly looking for the houses that had been there for 20 years. She hesitantly asks me "Have you seen the hawks?" "How about the crippled Chachalaca? Have you seen her? Is her baby ok?" I'm feeding them, Ginger, honestly, I am feeding them. The Whistling Ducks now come to the barn for corn, and the baby chicks are doing well, and I miss you guys!

The Simpson property becomes testament to progress within our City, another park, another place for folks to walk, to barbecue and a place for children to play that is safe and convenient.

Progress continues in McAllen, and while I know it is a good thing, I long for the days when I stood on the diving board and could see Ginger in the yard with the dogs, and Billy just pulling in with his old truck and cattle trailer.

Sadly, the *good old days* don't really have to be that long ago, I guess.

All The Things You Are

I'm just curious by nature, I guess, but when I saw them standing there, hand in hand, at the back of the meeting hall, as I had seen them a hundred times before, I wondered what their story was. They weren't EXACTLY teenagers, but you wouldn't have known it, as they talked, quietly, to each other, laughing occasionally, seeming to be in their own World.

The next day, I called his office and asked him to tell me the story of his "love affair" because I was so touched by their tenderness toward each other and their obvious devotion. I was delighted to find him enthusiastic to tell me about it, and her, and their life. The following is his story.

It wasn't as though it were a day unlike any other day that he had seen, but it was that he was seeing a *girl* unlike any other he had seen. To say that he stood and stared would be putting it mildly, he tells me, and it would be more appropriate to say that he stared with open mouth and glassy eyes. She attempted to not notice the young man, gaping, grinning and admiring from across the dining hall there at A & I, but it was just too obvious and she smiled behind her hand and whispered to her companions.

Of course, as it always is in a small area such as ours, a friend of his friend knew a friend of her friend, and as those things go, she came to McAllen to visit. He was "Johnny on the spot" offering to give her and her roommate a ride back to college at Kingsville. He couldn't take his eyes off of her and he found her to be more than beautiful, she was intelligent and quite spunky as well.

There was never a time that he didn't think she was perfect and **her** opinion that he was a bit on the adventuresome side for her, didn't, for once minute, detour him. He was his most winsome, convincing self when he finally asked her to accompany him to King's Inn for dinner, and he was surprised and delighted when she agreed to go. Sure, he had played the field a bit and kind of had the reputation of being a party animal, but when he appeared with her, his friends and comrades knew this was the thunderbolt. The best part? He knew from the beginning that she would be the love and light of his life .. The courtship began.

Please let me point out that while she wasn't all that sophisticated in the courtship process, she knew what she liked and she definitely liked this young man from the Valley.. The trip to meet her parents began with confidence; however, it was with a great deal of trepidation that the pair drove up that red clay road into Cotulla. Standing there on the front porch, he swears to me, stood Hoss Cartwright, arms folded across his massive chest (well, not exactly Hoss, but someone just as big and just as tough, it appeared our aspiring suitor). Of course, she was the apple of her dad's eye, and this scrawny little Valley boy just didn't measure up to dad's scrutiny! He, actually, had John Wayne in mind, but, then, you know dads. Her mom, now, thought that he was just wonderful - and that, maybe, just maybe she saw a sparkle of love in her little girls eyes..

Although they now argue who asked whom to marry whom, they both agree that they decided to marry somewhere along that road back from Cotulla to college at Kingsville. Two years later, they eloped and were married in the Pastor's study at the Second Baptist Church in Corpus Christi.

So, as love stories go, it has been a love story without end, they still attend every function together, he still adores her, and she still doesn't care that he's not John Wayne. Happy anniversary, John and Shirley - forty-four years of marriage never looked so good.

The Guys My Age

It's been a long summer... A summer where friends have died and I am forced to recall my Dad's statement "It used to be those old guys who were dying and now it's the guys MY age." I laughed when he said it, and didn't understand how he felt when he said it, but I now know.

The sense of loss– the loss of a friend, the loss of someone you admired, and the knowledge old age approaches quietly.... Yeah, Dad, it used to be the old guys dying– now it's the guys <u>MY</u> age... How different the mourning now, how difficult the mourning now and how very real the mourning now.

My friend Dave Andis died early summer from heart failure, I guess, and I felt sad for his loved ones, especially Kevin, his boy in college. Who could ever explain to Kev the real story on his beloved A & M. except, of course, Dave?

When my co-conspirator and fellow Lion, Bill Patterson, died, I went to his funeral and sang and clapped and felt overwhelming joy just over the story of his life. I miss him, my friend, Bill.

The firefighters rallied when Ex-Chief Johnny Economedes died, and as I walked up Closner Street there in Edinburg, with a couple of hundred firefighters and police officers and highway patrolman and citizens I felt the City's sense of loss. The fire trucks lined the streets, lights flashing, and marching, uniformed officers trailed along behind the hearse. The sun beat down on us with its usual late summer ferocity and I marveled at the hundreds standing there in the morning sun to bid farewell to Johnny. His life read like a storybook– the tales of his heroics and his sacrifices. He was true to every civic organization, being President of this one and Chairman of that one. He worked so very hard for his community, and was a hero on a month to month basis– and even in death, he turned out to be a hero. His final act of heroics? He donated his organs and skin to the Organ Donors bank. He helped a burn victim to heal, he helped a blind person to see and, perhaps, just perhaps, he saved another life or two along the way. So long, Johnny, your City of Edinburg will miss you, but we *all* will remember and admire you and the way you lived your life.

Leonel, our wonderful friend, Leonel. He wasn't supposed to die now. He had tried too hard, he had worked too long at getting well; he had set a goal, and he kept to it. He wasn't supposed to go yet. We weren't ready for it. He was proud that he had lost so much weight and had been walking and exercising–he said he <u>might</u> have to go back in for yet another heart "check", but he was (as usual) optimistic and cheerful.

He did give me some last minute instructions– (I was going for a Hospital Board meeting in San Francisco). "You have to go to Carmel– it is so beautiful– you will enjoy the ride, you will love the country– oh, and by the way, there is a little restaurant right outside the City limits– you have to stop there!" Leave it to our friend Leonel– he was knowledgeable– you name the subject, and he knew about it. From protocol in the Emergency Room and Risk Management for the Hospital to preparing the finest paella; to knowing the lay of the land from Brownsville to Corpus, Leonel knew it. He didn't flaunt it, but you darn well know that he <u>knew</u> it. (He knew there was a place outside Raymondville that "has the best lemon pie in the Valley" and was relentless until we went the 25 miles of bad road just to get to it.)

You'd have to know Leonel to know the singular joy he took in his life and his family. He and Linda were a team, and you'd see them at about every function, hand in hand. He greeted and was greeted by every person who knew him as though there were royalty in the group. Within that grand framework that was Leonel, beat a heart so very pure and so very kind, that perhaps, just perhaps, we *could* know him as a prince. Our friend, our confidant, our prince, Leonel Garza, how we miss him.

I hope that winter is uncreative in its wants this year, and leave the "old guys my age" here with us for another couple of years.

Weird Stuff

I was asking my friend, Rodd, the other day if he thought weird stuff happened to us— it appears that there is usually some major (or minor) occurrence that passes our way on a day to day basis. He was calm— " Sir, (he always calls me "Sir") it's because we are open to "stuff" happening to us," he said, philosophically, "most people aren't curious enough to check it out."

Busily deciphering this bit of information, while sitting across from him in his tree house, I noticed, for the first time, that he had phony birds sitting on the tree house rails. "Hey— what's with the birds, are they to scare away birds or to entice birds?" He just shrugged and said he liked them, "sort of like you like the sheep you have in your dining room." Oh yeah. Lann came clambering over the 9-foot fence that encircles Rodd's place and was about eye to eye with us before dismounting and marching up the incline into the tree house. Eager to get Lann into the conversation, I asked him "How come so many weird things happen to us, Lann?" He looked puzzled "What do you mean "weird"? I never noticed weird stuff happening to us." "Hey, Rodd, when are you putting the slide in for your tree house— after I put MY slide in my tree house, it was a lot better."

Conversation dwindled on the weird stuff and we talked some politics and some Koi fish tales, how I hadn't fed mine for two months, and when

I did, they ignored the food. Rodd said that his had had heat strokes so he put 2 ten-pound bags of ice in the pond every day. And that the giant hand that the water pumped over into his pond had become too mossy of late and he'd have to scrub it down later, because it was too slippery for his iguana to sun upon.

On my way home, I swung into the Simpson's place when I noticed Ginger out gardening. "Hey Ginger! You know I have been thinking that weird stuff always seems to happen to my friends and me– what do you think?" She looked puzzled, but shrugged and asked me to come in and see her Whistling Duck, "Ducky". "You know, I taught him to fly by taking his stuffed bunny and played like IT was flying!" She happily called out "Ducky" and gave a whistle– a responding whistle sounded from the pen in the corner of the yard. Sure enough, Ducky was delighted to see us and sprang to her shoulder and nestled in. When Ducky's real mom had flown the coop, he was left on his own, and Ginger became his surrogate mom.

(I remembered the time that I found the baby rabbit trapped in the barn, and Ginger had cared for him until– <u>until</u> he got loose in the upstairs bedroom. By the time he resurfaced, he was old enough to be turned outside on his own!) The baby woodpecker I stopped traffic to rescue on Main Street went to Ginger as well, and he still lives somewhere there in the trees at the Simpson home. Griggs Search and Rescue wouldn't be worth a hoot without the Nurse Ginger Home for unloved babies, so it's a good team effort.

When I arrived home, Darrell (my two black chickens with the white shock of feathers on their heads) met me at the walkway with their buddy, Ginny the Guinea. The four of us walked to the barn with me scolding Darrell for being out of the pasture fence and Ginny for being so vocal. Cowboy, my parrot, must have heard the commotion, because he immediately stated calling out "Mister Donut– Mister Donut" from the interior of the house.

Perched on his doggie TV platform, Slick was outside to greet me, and I earnestly asked him "Slick, do YOU think my friends and I have weird things happen to us?" He didn't look too concerned, so I guess I'll quit worrying about it.

The Christmas Babies

I guess I will always think of them as the Christmas babies. Not because they were born at Christmas, but because my friends told me at their Christmas party that they were *expecting* a baby. And, sure enough, when I arrived at the hospital to see "the" baby in June, there *they* were— twin babies, a boy and a girl. Art, of course, was disgusting in his roll as new dad and had the door to the room attired with both pink and blue wreaths and was discussing football plays as well as ballet lessons that were in store for some time in the future. Barbara glowed from her bed, eyes never leaving the twin cradles that held "my" Christmas babies.

Yesterday, I went to call upon those Christmas babies and we spent a harrowing (for me) hour in the toy room— for, while it seems like yesterday that I stood, spellbound, staring at those tiny bundles in the hospital, my Christmas babies are now 2 ½ years old. What a great age they are. They are filled with an enormous amount of energy and while I sat on the floor in the midst of the games, musical toys and jumping "stuff" they tackled each job with the dedication of master craftsman. Trey played some musical gadget for me and did the appropriate jerks and head rolls to let me know he, in fact, got "down" to the music. Aubrey, on the other hand, lugged book after book to my lap and acquainted me with all the nuances of the tab pulling and the hidden folds that showed hiding panda bears and sleeping kitties.

These two munchkins, so alike, but so totally unlike, took my breath away there on the toy room floor yesterday. Trey was by far the more serious of the two, with a sometimes eyebrow furrow as he figures out one toy or another. Aubrey, is 'way more silly and far more cuddly (but isn't that the job of the "woman" of the pair?) and had to take my hand to lead me to some of her finer treasures.

I remember my daughter Tracy at this age and the particular glee she took in fitting and refitting her "pop" beads, and the simplicity of her play. Now, Trey and Aubrey know how to insert the video into the TV and do the "wiggle" dance with their favorite stars. They know how to punch the different colors on their computer games and play different songs. The instruments of play may have changed over the years, but I see the children much the same. Barbara tells me that the children can play for hours in a cardboard box in which a particularly nice toy arrived, and tenting under the covers at bedtime brings about the same giggles and wrestling that it did back when we were children.

This is the season when prayers are answered and I happen to know a home where prayers are given each evening at bedtime that simply give thanks for the miracle of these "other" Christmas babies.

Jacque's Mom

When my friend Jacque's mom died on the Tuesday following Thanksgiving it set in motion many serious sit-downs between us; an early morning breakfast, or a mid-afternoon coke, to speak about the bond that exists between mothers and daughters. A love so completely binding that it leaves us feeling guilty when we, in fact, lose that loved one.

Zella, Jacque's mom, was 87 when she died, and while Jacque knew it was mom's time to go, the fact of the matter was, while Jacque was ready in her head for mom to pass on, her heart just wasn't ready. We laughed, through our tears, about Zella. She was a liberated woman 'way before liberated women were cool. She was a City Commissioner in Harper, Kansas, and the first woman on the Commission EVER.

She had weathered many personal storms that had driven her and Jacque to an even more inseparable union, and through the years, the bond strengthened. When she became ill prepared to live alone up in the cold country, she came to the Valley to be with Jeff and Jacque. While the years passing simply meant she had begun to require additional care, the family unit remained safe and secure. She had moved from the family home to an assisted living home, where she, of course, owned her own little apartment. Then, the gentle decline from caring for herself went to requiring an available person to attend to her just about full time. She hated it and pretty much hated all that went with this "old age" business—and was the first to let you know about it.

She was up to the minute on the political news I'll tell you, and had some pretty definite ideas about who was doing what out there. She did acquire what Jacque and I would refer to as the "fat person alert" after she passed 80, and would point out any person slightly overweight. She made us laugh, this feisty little old lady! I remember standing around down in the emergency room after she had had some mishap, her white curls were standing up with indignity from too much bed time, and she cussed and discussed the merits of old age and all the infirmities that went with it.

Zella went back to Nash, Oklahoma, that week following Thanksgiving. According to her wishes, she was cremated and is now nestled between the graves of her own parents.

Jacque and I talk about our moms a lot. We do laugh a bit at the idiosyncrasies that they had acquired over those last years and felt fairly smug that we would not burden OUR daughters with anything like that. Then we asked our daughters— and they said we *already* had established weird and unusual behaviors that tended to shock and amaze them. Go figure!!

Just Passing Through

I guess that I never really understood before. Sure, I had heard of it, but to actually live it, was quite another matter.

Last Saturday I went to a fun funeral. I know, I know. It doesn't seem possible, but when I walked away from the Baptist Church there on Ash Street, I knew something special had just happened to me, and a whole church load of people. We felt good, and we had just, for heaven's sake, said "Goodbye" to an old friend.

Sure, there were a lot of tears slipping unnoticed down cheeks and quite a few sniffles from, not only, the parishioners but the choir as well. Yet every face had a smile, a look of understanding and a certain degree of– "yeah, we knew him– he was **our** guy– and he **was** great!"

His son, with a voice clear and sweet, sang to his father. We watched in amazement as he addressed the words, to the casket, and the man who lay within. He told of a man who had raised his children to love humanity and to share the joy of living with their community. He sang of a man who was unstoppable in his beliefs and in his devotion to family, friends and his church. He sang of his father, our friend, Bill.

The choir sang, and the soloists, faces wreathed with joy, sang of happy times and the journey of a man, who believed, and his ultimate destination. The honorary speakers, friends of long standing, told us stories that we didn't know about him, our fellow Lion, and we marveled that he had been our friend, also.

For such an ordinary guy; he had kind of a mischievous look to him that always made me want to ask him what he was up to. He was as silly as a kid sometimes, but his calm demeanor at others, made you want to stop and listen.

He was a Lion's Club member in my Lion's Club, and he sat in front and to the right of the speaker's table, and listened attentively to every speaker. Now I'm certainly not going to tell you that all of our speakers have received the same courtesy from all of our members, but you could count on Bill to give everyone the courtesy and respect that they deserved.

Every once in a while Bill would bring Betty to Lions– just to give us a little "class" he said, but I think that he just liked to have her along, just cuz' he just liked to have her along. We all, of course, liked it when she came, because it gave us the opportunity to badger Bill about one thing and another - much to her amusement. But, then again, Bill had been a Lions Club member for 50+ years, so nothing we did could ever **really** shock her!

We went to a fun funeral yesterday, we wished our friend, Bill, Godspeed on his continued journey to a better place. We went to a proud funeral yesterday, a funeral that celebrated the life of our friend– we went to mourn our friend, Bill, but ended up just praising him.

I'll miss him, my friend, but, after yesterday, I can't mourn his passing, I will continue celebrating his life, by, perhaps, being just a little more compassionate, a little kinder and a whole lot more understanding. God blessed **us**, Bill, by sharing you. You shall remain forever in our hearts.

The Donut Shop Lovers

The donut shop on South 10th Street was where they would rendezvous those many years ago. They would come in for coffee and a donut every afternoon. He would drive HIS car, and she would drive HER car, always parking some spaces apart in the parking lot. We, coffee servers, talked behind our hands about them— envisioning a clandestine relationship going on right there in our very own Donut Shop - while they sat in the corner booth, by themselves. The "meeting" took place at approximately the same time every day, and we would wait to see them come in from different directions.

They were such a handsome couple, he, with the silvering hair, and she dressed in the most up to date fashion, with (always) matching shoes and purse. We decided that they, of course, were having a love affair. Lots of time they sat for an hour, talking softly, laughing at some undisclosed joke or intimate gossip. They even (gasp) held hands occasionally as they walked to the door to leave, and we questioned the wisdom of such an act right there in broad daylight.

The years passed rapidly, and they continued their afternoon coffee and donut ritual. While the girls and I knew them simply as Jessie and Mary Lou, their "love affair" turned out to be the ultimate love affair. For, you see, they had been married at that time for almost 20 years!!

From that day forward, while I knew the lovers who sat in the corner of the donut shop to be Jessie and Mary Lou, I could never think of them as anything other than our "donut shop lovers". That was some 30 years ago, and over these years, I have become friends with my 'donut shop lovers". I continue to see them, holding hands and speaking quietly to each other at different functions. They arrive together, he guides her with his hand in the small of her back, to the chair he will pull out and she has been known to reach up and carefully adjust his silver hair.

He is still the guy with the silver hair and she is the petite little lady with the great up-to-date fashions and the matching shoes and purse. While thirty years have passed since I first saw them there in the donut shop, the love story goes on between Mary Lou and Jessie Trevino.

They are celebrating their 50 wedding anniversary this month, and I smile to think of them and the love they share have shared over these past years.

Dad And Me

She looked like a beautiful little gnome sitting there—fork midway to her mouth—"Tell her the story about the trip with your dad, Dan— it's such a wonderful story!" She was so childlike and eager, that I looked closely at my friend sitting there looking with sparkling eyes at her husband—"Come on Dan, tell her."

He did the "oh gosh" thing, but leaned back in his chair to tell me the story that I like to refer to as "Dad and Me".

It appears that Dan was, in stature, and in talent much like his Mom, a diminutive, athletic dancer, not like dad, who was full time military and a rousing 6'2" perfectionist. Dan's talents lay in the acrobatic, the athletic, and the many things, in which, a boy, driven by the will to succeed, could hope to excel. Diving and swimming were his forte' and he spent his high school years winning against the local competition and just plain being the best that he could be.

While dad was never *really* a front line supporter, he never discouraged his boy from athletics, and was proud of him in the way that some parents are proud (bragging to friends, dropping hints to acquaintances, and never telling his kid, first hand, how proud he really was). So, consequently, when the trip to look at college, there in his senior year of high school, came to pass, it was Dan and dad and a long road trip.

Coming back from the Military College where Dan was going to attend, a side trip to the University of Michigan was a spur of the moment decision, the beautiful campus beckoning and there, lo and behold, the welcoming sign on campus announced "Free Style Dive Competition" – Saturday and Sunday. When dad said "How about it, Son, should we take a look?" Dan was as surprised and excited as any 17-year-old would be when "dad" makes such a move toward camaraderie - and, on that Friday afternoon they walked shoulder to shoulder into the natatorium listening to the familiar sounds of boys diving and swimming and enthusiastic competition. -

Dan was mystified when his dad asked him about "that" dive and "that one over there" – and could he do those? Sure, he had done them, he said, but it had been 9 months since the competition there at High School, and he, possibly, was a little rusty. Be that as it may, Dan leaned forward from the bleachers watching and admiring the divers and swimmers, and, perhaps, in some small way, wishing he were out there.

Dad took a brief sabbatical from the bleacher seats, but when he returned, he indicated that it was time to get a move on, and Dan, jumped to his feet and followed to the car and the long road home. But home was not the destination, the local sporting goods store was, and when Dan quizzically asked his dad– "what's going on here?" he said it was time to get him suited up for the Dive Competition.

It appears that when dad had spent those moments away from the bleachers on that Friday afternoon, he had been talking to the Coach back at Dan's high school. He, himself, had been appointed as Dan's coach, and could (and did) enter him in the College Dive Competition there at the University of Michigan...

It was a week-end for fathers and sons according to Dan– with his dad sitting alone on the east side of the bleachers, quietly applauding his "team", Dan dived like he had never dived before. Together that evening, in the Motel, with dim light burning into the night, they mapped out Dan's strategy for the coming day.

Now the local champion, Glenn Nugie, surrounded by his league of worshippers, had heard that the new guy was in town, but he never broke a sweat– heck, Dan was just a kid and heck, he hadn't dived for months. No sweat, he's no competition. And when Glen stepped up to the diving board for each dive (practice or otherwise) the bleachers erupted into cheers and shrieks of joy, except, of course, for the east bleacher where Dan's "coach" stood quietly applauding.

The competition was fierce that day, and at the end of the first day's session, Dan was behind Glen by 30 points– in third place, and glad to be there! Glen, on the other hand, prowled among his gang of merry men and told them not to worry, tomorrow would be the telling tale, and Dan would be left far behind. His body should be aching (after all, he hadn't dived for 9 months) and his will should be diminished.

A new day dawned and the diving gladiators went one on one– Glen's lead dwindling after each dive. Dan did notice that, by now, his dad no longer stood alone there on the east bleachers– and was acting pretty wild and crazy for a full Bird Colonel

It was time for the finale'– and Dan was ready for the double twist– the final dive of the competition. He and Glen were now neck'n neck, points almost equal; the crowd was quiet and apprehensive and even dad, standing ramrod straight in typical military fashion, looked ready to jump into the air with anticipation.

Then this 17-year old boy/man sailed off the board and into the air and, as effortlessly as breathing, went through his double twist performance and sliced into the pool with scarcely a ripple. Needless to say, the crowd went wild, when the scorekeepers held up the winning numbers and Dan became the first ever State Champion for his high school.

It was just a weekend road trip for a kid and his father, a weekend trip that determined the adult relationship between two men, one, simply younger. Two equals now in some crazy, wonderful conspiracy that joined them forever in a scenario that only they would ever understand and remember. And it was good.

Letter to Larry

I have been thinking a lot about you over these past two weeks, Larry. In fact, you haven't been very far from my mind and heart, since the weekend that we, here in McAllen, found out that your father had died. I didn't know your father, and, while you and I are friends, I don't know why this has been lingering on the fringes of my thoughts for all of these days.

Something about a father and a son - two grown men now, the rules of childhood no longer apply. Neither being the leader nor the follower. Two equals whom the bonds of the love of a father and son bind, yes, but closeness that only deep friendship can bring.

In those formative years, some 30 years ago, it was dad who directed, instructed and reasoned with you; a young man, who, he knew in his heart, was just like he was at that age. You wavered between thinking that he was rather old-fashioned and unrelenting, and, yet, in some crazy fashion, your very own hero.

Your parent's ranch is the sanctuary where you go to revitalize yourself and your family - a sanctuary where the keeper of the gates has always been your Father. You no longer viewed him as old-fashioned and unrelenting, but historical and disciplined.

I can picture those late evening talks, your mom and your family off to bed, and you and dad, leaning forward, eagerly sharing those thoughts that only friends and soul mates can share. Your trials of running a program as large as the one in McAllen, the accomplishments and the missteps. Him offering suggestions and giving parallel situations that he had had during his lifetime. Him walking you through the ranch and the happenings over the past months since last you came.

Somehow over these many years it has remained the same, mom, dad, the ranch, and the area surrounding it. The same ranch where your grandfather lived and your father grew to manhood and eventually married and raised his family. That family loved the land, where, perhaps, someday your grandchildren will play in the barn and you will walk the fields with your children.

For now, you will walk where you once walked together, and know that much of that vision you shared has become a reality. Constantly remind yourself that you are but an extension of him, and how very fortunate you were to have had each other for those many, many years. The pride you knew having him as a father? Well, think how very, very proud he must have been of you.

No one will ever doubt that you will continue to miss him and long for the late night confabs and walks through the green pastures. Life goes on, however, and you remember him gratefully. Now the baton is passed, the sanctuary becomes yours, and YOU become the keeper of the gates. Life goes on.

Monica's Angels

I didn't attend Monica's funeral today. I wanted to go, I was dressed to go, but I just couldn't go. I wanted to be there so that I could hug her parents and tell them that she had gone to a better place that God would watch over her and that everything would be OK. But, as I sat there, on the edge of my bed, with shoes in hand, I knew I could never go.

This courageous child, (she *was* a child, you know, not the courageous adult we all came to know as Monica), this beautiful child who had a lifetime, not only in front of her, but also, unfortunately, behind her as well, rose above herself to influence an entire generation. To assure those of us of an older generation, that strength and courage do not necessarily come with age, but with character. Influencing the ill to persevere, to move forward with dignity. And, above all else, her generation - the *Monica Generation* I will forever call it - the compassionate, giving, loyal and steadfast generation - who will spend the rest of their lives remembering. Remembering that there **was** a Monica - not just the girl next door, or the smart girl in Civics, but a generation-changer - *our* Monica.

She will be a lifetime inspiration to her classmates; will they not speak of her courage and compassion and beauty when they are raising their own children? Will they not use her as the yardstick to measure the rest of their lives? Will a day pass that they don't recall how she stood tall and unafraid, when those around her cried and were afraid for her?

I am sorry I didn't attend the funeral, I, selfishly, preferred to think of her in *my* text, short hair blowing around her face, eyes sparkling, laughing (and making her friends laugh as well). The Monica who fought the tough fight, and won the battles, the Monica who will remain forever in our hearts.

I am grateful for her innocence, for her being her own person, for fighting every step of the way. For loving her parents and for loving her friends— weren't we all privileged to know her?

The Barbecue Guys

The guys are working now (I like to think of them as "the guys", a team, - - one for all– all for one). I think of them as "my guys" to be truthful, but in reality, they are their own "guys" and march to the drum beat that inspires them. In this particular case, and on this particular morning, they are Lion's Club barbecue guys– they have been at the fires since 3 AM and will probably remain there until 3 PM.

They are a hardworking, dedicated three-some and the challenge of the barbecue whips them along as assuredly as though they had a master– which, of course, they don't. Each is set to their particular task– Gene doing much of the up front legwork; purchase the chickens, buy the ingredients and haul the various bags and baggage into the Palmer Pavilion hut. Mike, early on, begins mixing the secret barbecue sauce, and Manny hauls the wood and begins to set up the fires. The cutting, chopping, and up front stuff begins immediately and 8 hours later the actual barbecuing. Gene's famous beans are critiqued by the other 2/3rds of the guys– a pinch of salt more, perhaps just a drop more of picante– a taste here– a test there– finally– perfect.

When the rest of us arrive in the late evening, we are immediately directed to cabbage or carrots– Theda and I mix the couple hundred pounds of coleslaw with Gene supervising– "No!– More sugar, less vinegar, try some celery salt!" Mike inspects the chickens as the "rookie" guys help out— and Manny just plain keeps his eyes on his work and cuts and slices, raising his head to occasionally grin at the antics of the "outsiders" who stop by to help.

By 9:30 AM— as I head out there to help again, I know that they really don't need me as the hut will be clean, and smelling good and huge pans of chicken are being pulled from the fires— the magic sauce being lavishly painted on each chicken half. The guys will be fairly grubby, with stubs of beards, and many tomatoey handprints on their apron fronts at this point, but they will be happy and uncomplaining as the rest of the Club members drift in.

By 11:30 AM most Lions have arrived and go immediately to begin their task. After Bill Meyers and I put the chicken into the "to-go boxes", Jeff and Les on opposite sides of the assembly line put in the beans, Theda, Sandy, Jack, Eddie, Joanne, Bill— all assembly line workers— onions, coleslaw, pickles— fresh white bread. We're a team, and we can put out the plates, let me tell you!

The guys now alternate between supervisory positions and helping — hauling the hot, heavy pans filled with steaming chicken, promptly bringing the tubs filled to the brim with coleslaw (that we can't even lift), gathering the dirty pans and washing them as we go. They never stop moving, and I marvel at their efficiency, they never once complain, but I do occasionally see them rolling their eyes when one of the newcomers sits down and eats before "paying their dues" of hard work. Manny keeps everyone laughing; he's the spark-plug that keeps us all running!

Outside, the members who take the plates to the cars, back and forth between Hut and auto— smile and talk to each "customer". Ben stands, alone, up by the gate, to direct and to see if, perhaps, they need another few tickets. (Ben worked late into the night with the guys this year and as future President of our Club, he gets to be involved in **all** of the jobs.)

It's all over by 2 PM, and most of the members drift off again, leaving the guys to continue with the clean up. A couple other diehards stay 'til the bitter end, to help with sweeping, cleaning and hauling, but, until the last pan is washed, until the last coal is out, the "guys" remain.

I'm proud to be affiliated with my favorite civic group, the Lions Club, and, you know what? I am proud that I am affiliated with the guys, Gene, Manny, Mike, who make it their charge to make our barbecue a success. I hope, when we send that check to the Crippled Children's Camp we all remember those unsung heroes who stoke the fires and clean the pans. For in each Club out there, there are those who make these things seem easy and fun. My guys, that's what they do. Thanks, guys!

River Song

Robin and I became neighbors in 1991 when I moved to a small farm on the outskirts of McAllen. She and her family lived directly in a house on four acres immediately behind my home. It was a natural state of affairs for Robin and I to become friends. Being single parent, with my only daughter living in Athens, Greece, and Robin, an enthusiastic, almost teen, spending too much time by herself, with working parents and older siblings, she and I naturally gravitated to each other.

On the weekend of the 4th of July, I had asked her parents if she could accompany friends and I to the Hill Country and, of course, they agreed. We plotted all of the way up there, to rent "tubes" and go down the river. The other adults in our party declined, but we were adamant and they dropped us off to spin our way down the river. The thought never occurred to me that this could be a dangerous adventure for us, we simply piled onto the tubes and away we went.

It was a two-hour trek on the tubes, and I was blissfully unaware of the dangers that lurked below my inner tube and me. We reached the end of the trip without mishap, and when I saw that the other "tubers" were stepping off their tubes, I, also stepped off. In some crazy set of circumstances, my tube shot up and over me, projecting me into the swirling, deep part of the river. I sank like a rock, only to come struggling back to the surface, knowing, full well, this could and, probably, would be my last tube ride. Robin sat, perched on her tube looking fearfully for me and I surfaced with the panic of any person who cannot swim - "Robin - I can't swim!"

She never looked right or left, she dove without hesitation into the River. I was back under by then, and I felt her small hands come under my back and she lifted me to the surface. I am a fairly large, middle age woman, but this young lady repeatedly went below the surface to hold me above the water - she admonished me "Be calm, don't struggle" and we both called for help. It was, I assume a typical 4th of July Weekend - hundreds of college students, coolers of beer and much gaiety, and we were ignored. Finally, an older bystander plunged in and brought the inner tube to us and we dragged ourselves to the bank.

I, of course, was ill from the enormous amount of water I consumed, and was trembling so hard I could barely stand. Robin stood, holding my hand, face white, and eyes fearful.

"You'll be ok, it's ok, don't worry, you're ok now." The horror of it hit me then - SHE could have died. I said "Robin, Robin, you could have drowned in this mess" and she said, like the champion she is, "Phyllis, I wasn't coming out without you." My friend, my hero, Robin Moore.

My Chief

He's my Chief, up there in the Hospital, my personal Chief, my friend and my pal; and in my head there is a film playing scenes of this friendship that started so long ago.

The night that I first got to know him was when we all dressed up and became the stars of "Dick Tracy" for our local Police "Night Out"; Chief was decked out in an old fashioned uniform, bow tie, hat and the obligatory handkerchief to wipe his brow. I laughed just looking at him, and believe me when I tell you while he was no Mel Gibson; he took his acting seriously and played the part to the hilt.

Actually, I knew *of* him when I owned the Donut Shops– because when he became Chief, he wouldn't let the Officers come in for free coffee and donuts anymore. I sent word to his office, and he called me back to tell me that while Officers were on duty, he couldn't allow free anything– and that, pretty much, was that. There is never any gray area for my Chief. Things are pretty much right– or they are wrong.

Slowly over these past 14 years that I have been on the Commission, my Chief and I have become friends, we go out to lunch together occasionally, and we always take turns paying the check. We try to avoid talking about City "stuff", but he **has** been known to praise his wife, Margie, and, wonder, aloud, how she puts up with his long hours (and I think to myself, his gruff manner). He has told me of the love he has for his children, and told me many tales about Josh, his grandson. I tell him about my daughter, Tracy and my dog and he talks about law enforcement in general– his trips to Quantico and the classes he has taught.

I know he spends his idle time doing woodwork- building altars: that he has an Asian garden and that he has very poor luck with his pets. I know my Chief in a personal way although I have never set foot in his home. I know my Chief in a solemn and respectful way because I see his heart and it is good.

The time moves ahead rapidly now, years passing, and our friendship continuing and we are asked to go to Washington, D. C. to pick up grant money for which he has applied. Chief's and my journey to the White House was most assuredly a surprise! We were just a couple of rookies, guessing that something good was about to happen and, sure enuf it did. We pressed the flesh there in the Oval Office and we received a $3.8 million dollar grant to boot.

When the presentation was over, Chief ambled off across the driveways, coat over his arm, and I walked along behind him. I was thinking because of this Chief of ours, the citizens of McAllen were safer by 28 officers; because of him, our City coffers were fuller by enough money to fund a crime prevention program. Because of his initiative and his love for this City, he, one person, had made all of this happen.

We stood out on the street in front of the White House– just the two of us, two good old boys from South Texas, and we simply stared at each other. We were sweating and rumpled, and my feet were killing me. I guess it hit us at the same time, we started laughing and gave each other a high five, and walked away from our day in the sun.

And now, standing outside of the hospital gazing up into faceless windows, I pray for my Chief, and I pray for his family. They (and he) know that I love him, my friend, my pal, my hero, My Chief.

Animal Love

I was the little girl who had the dog follow her home; the little girl who "found" the kitties and who called the police department when a horse was being abused. The little girl who slept with a white dog named "Bugs" and cried a river when "Bugs" died of old age at 15.

The dogs and horses and the birds and the animals that I have loved and cared and fussed over through these past 70 years would fill a book. The animals rescued by the side of the road and the stalls filled with sorrowful remnants of old horses, goats and chickens harbor but a small window into my love of animals.

It's actually pretty simple – you love them, and, eventually, they love you. I like the simplicity of it!

Puppy love

Looking at my "puppy" lately, I find that, in fact, he is really no longer a "puppy", but an old doggie. He now has gray hair on his muzzle; the white and the gray have faded together into that distinguished old doggie mask that we all know so well.

He has been my roommate and companion for 11 years now - I remember the day that Tracy brought him to me - it was the day before Mother's Day, 1987. He weighed an amazingly light 12 pounds. He was as cuddly and soft, as he was mischievous and destructive. He came tumbling across the floor there at Ms Carol's and grabbed the leg of my Levis and it was chaos from that point forward.

He did glean a certain reputation within my circle of friends - beware of the teeth of steel (needles, during THAT period, galvanized nails later) - he chewed and he tore, he dragged and he plundered. It was a constant curiosity at the Dr. Gray's office to see what he had eaten THAT week.

Legs from tables, chairs, remote controls, shoes - aah yes, he loved shoes with a fervor that can only be matched by my own. When he ate the heating pad - leaving only the thermostat, slightly gnawed, but recognizable, he became the darling of the Doctors there at the Clinic. He was never sick from his excursions, and even when my friend Jack Cawood brewed up a concoction of cinnamon, garlic and chili and I used it to paint the legs of the chairs, he ate away.

Slick is an American Staffordshire Terrier, fierce of countenance, and a dead ringer for the much-maligned Pit Bull. However, he is close to double their size - a dainty 78 to 85 pounds (depending if I cut the fat from his chicken when I prepare his chicken and rice dinner). He is, without a doubt, the most beautiful dog I have ever seen - his carriage is regal, and his eyes are intelligent and clear. There is no waste of motion with Slick, muscles ripple and coat shines brightly as he attends to his "guard duty" there at the house.

My favorite story about him addresses what I like to think of as his "intellect". He was as happy as any child that "Mom" was home for the day and while I cleaned the fish tank, he romped in and out the doors with me. Occasionally, I would go outside and stir up the gravel and swoosh the hose up and down in the bucket of fish tank gravel. The last time I went out - the hose was gone! It was one of those - Hey! - What? Where? Why? Upon following the hose from its connection, I found that, in fact, it wasn't lost, it was extremely found. He had taken it in through his doggie door, and there he sat, in the middle of my bedroom, elbow deep in water, and hose still running. It was wag, wag, splash, splash. He was exceedingly happy, and, might I add, proud? I laughed until I was sick, pulled the bedding off the bed and mopped up the damage. My puppy, my dog.

While he is territorial, to, perhaps, a fault, he keeps me from harm's way by keeping possums, rats, snakes, and, unfortunately, cats a scarce commodity at my home as well as my little house at the Island. On the positive, I wander the beach a various hours of the morning and evening, and he runs by my side, and I feel safe. There at our farm, he sleeps at the end of the bed and the slightest noise sends him flying into the yard to snuff and woof. My partner, my protector.

Friday evening, when I get home, he romps and plays like a puppy, running back and forth to the back door and the car - long ago, I realized he knew it was Island time. It must be his way of telling me - "hey it's only one day early - lets go TODAY." He knows and I know he knows the days. My playmate, my traveler.

I hold his giant head in my hands sometimes, looking into those clear brown eyes, and worry what I will do when he is gone. He doesn't range as far on the beach as he did 10 years ago, but, then again, neither do I. I do love this mountain of a gentle dog, his silliness and his seriousness, and I shall miss him fiercely when he's gone. My friend, my companion.

The City Slicker

Slick began an uneasy truce with old age about a year ago, I guess. His venturing up the beach was much slower, and his romps with his tug of war much quicker. He could still snap up that little tail on the pool sweep in a heartbeat, however, and his last possum kill was barely five months ago. He watched "doggie TV" from the corner of the fence, and could spot a dog across the yard and across the street and give notice to "stay away" in his best big dog bark.

Actually, he had quit noticing the lesser evils that plagued him there in the back yard, Funny Chicken and her brood of six baby guineas usually came in to poke among the flowers and palm stumps, early of a morning, but he pretty much ignored them. Now that's not to say he wouldn't have given chase had they but crossed his path, but, to go out of the way– nah. Several small rabbits would hop just out of his vision, as he happily walked around the pool and back into the house.

When he started losing the hair on his whip of a tail, I gathered him to go in to see Dr. Gray, and see just what the problem was– a series of blood tests simply said that the old liver in my old doggie was starting to fail. He took his pills with relish– stuck in the gooey center of a spoon of peanut butter– and never missed a day. When he staggered there by the pool two weeks ago, I hurriedly rushed him to Dr. Gray, knowing my old dog was deteriorating as each day passed. Dr. Gray said, perhaps the dizziness caused by a weakening heart. More pills, and many more tears.

I prayed nightly that I wouldn't have to make his life and death decision and asked God to take him in his sleep, when it was time, to spare me. However, as the days passed, he seemed to feel good– took his pills and lay at my feet every day and slept on the foot of the bed every night. Why just last night, after his bath, he galloped by the couch with his prized toy -

About a year ago, I wrote an article "Puppy Love"– about him and the camaraderie and love that we had shared for eleven years. In the final paragraph I said "I hold his giant head in my hands sometimes, looking into those clear brown eyes, and worry what I will do when he is gone." "I love this mountain of a gentle dog, his silliness and his seriousness, and I shall miss him fiercely when he's gone. My friend, my companion."

Slick died last night, in his sleep, in the cool evening air by the pool and I shall miss him fiercely. Adios, gentle friend, you go to a better place. Slick Griggs– March 18, 1987– June 20, 1999.

Little Dog Lost

I first saw the flyer at my business - "MISSING DOG - PLEASE HELP US FIND GIZMO" a picture of obviously happier times accompanied it, with a little boy sitting with a little dog - and a stick-on note attached to the bottom said "Phyllis, this is your friend Paul Garcia's dog - would you mind putting this poster up in your window?" Of course, I didn't mind and posted it immediately - wondering what possibly could have become of the little dachshund - he appeared to be very happy with his circumstances, perched on Paul Garcia's little boy's lap.

I wondered of dognappers and hit and run drivers and the fate of Gizmo.

The search went on and on and the kids went from door to door inquiring if anyone had seen a little dog - a friendly little dog that answered to the name of Gizmo. The newspaper ad brought a few calls from well wishers, but it appeared that Gizmo was gone. The number of dogs and cats killed by the side of the road is incredible, and I quizzed Paul about the wandering habits of Gizmo - he told me the little dog stayed close to home and rarely ventured away from the porch - and as the weeks passed, I, too, became convinced that the dog was gone forever.

Paul Garcia's dog really wasn't a close acquaintance - I had, perhaps, seen him at the window of Paul and Sandy's house, and maybe I had heard him barking when we rang the door bell - but we, actually, weren't old friends. As I gradually learned about Gizmo, I discovered he was funny and playful and the slightest bit overweight for a young dachshund, he had, of course, a favorite toy and sometimes, in the dark of the night, crept into the bed of George Garcia, Paul and Sandy's youngest son.

Gizmo Garcia had disappeared in mid October and as November sped by, I had almost quit asking Paul about the continuing search for the wayward Gizmo. The day before Thanksgiving was a hectic day in the Garcia neighborhood - the next door neighbors had guests in from out of town - when they walked to their old car in the back yard, awaiting parts, and opened the hood - there wedged inside the battery housing was the skeletal body of Paul Garcia's dog - one of the men cried out - "My God! There's a dead dog in here!" At the sound of his voice, a frail ear moved and there was a faint stirring from within the tiny body. With Gizmo wrapped in a towel, it was a race to the Veterinary - and then, as they say, the rest is history.

Immediately after school, George Garcia stood respectfully outside of a pristine white doggy hospital room and softly cried the name "Gizmo" and amidst the drip tubes and healing devices attached to Gizmo, the little dog struggled to get to his feet. For although six full weeks had passed, with no explainable logic why he was alive, Gizmo Garcia recognized the sound of his master's voice, and lived. You see, as it turned out, Paul Garcia's dog really was Georgie Garcia's dog and as of this writing, he is alive and well, and playing with his toys and sometimes sneaking into George's bed late in the night. And it was, indeed, a thankful Thanksgiving.

Good Girl

She probably wasn't all <u>that</u> much of a prize twelve years ago, when Tracy found her. She was skinny and injured— whoever had put the wire around her neck surely knew that it would grow into her skin, but, perhaps, they just didn't care. She appeared to be very hungry, as she nosed through each tiny scrap beside the dumpster.

Her survival instincts were terrific, however, and she seemed almost gay as she scurried around in the papers and trash. A portion of bread here and a French-fry there— what more could a starving, little dog require? Well, perhaps, all she really needed was what we all need over time, someone to care. And there staring down at her from her car window was Tracy, scarcely out of college, just out on her own and alone. She immediately retrieved the little dog and dubbed her "Squiggles".

A partnership was formed that day— a dog and her girl: a partnership based on the minimum requirements: love, respect and equality (and, of course, room, board and doggie treats). Tracy was just beginning her adult life at that juncture, moving into the new apartment there in Dallas, working and coming home to a previously empty house. Squiggs moved in and immediately began fulfilling her part of the requirements and loved Tracy with all her doggie heart.

When Trace accepted work with the Government, it required a move to D.C. and, of course, Squiggs moved with her. Car rides, airplane rides, they meant not the slightest inconvenience to Squiggs— she went, uncomplaining, to crate or to front seat with the same ease, and she was happy. Her new destination would require immediate research of the neighborhood and an obligatory sniff at the dumpsters (a carry over from her poverty stricken past). She had a funny little skip that tickled us no end and she hopped and skipped her way into every heart that she came across.

When they moved to Amman, Jordan, we worried about Squiggs— the long flight, the stopovers in New York and in Frankfort and other obvious perils that befall crate bound animals. She arrived in Amman, hale and hearty, tail wagging, with the anticipation of new neighborhoods and dumpsters to research. This was during the Gulf War period, and Tracy worried herself sick over the fact that evacuation was discussed daily there in the Embassy. She feared that she would go directly from Embassy to plane and be asked to leave Squiggs. (She of course, never entertained this as a serious option, I knew that she would stay there, herself. before ever leaving her roommate, Squiggs.) As it turned out, evacuation did occur, but Squiggs was hurriedly packed up and returned home with Tracy.

They were recalled to Amman several months later where they remained for another year. After that, a trip to D.C., a new neighborhood, a new dumpster and they were on to Athens, Greece. What a team they were (when I sent Barbara Bush beads to Squiggs for Christmas that year, she was the bell of the Marine Ball) and Tracy looked pretty darned good herself. The sights they saw, their walks among the ruins of history from the Dead Sea to the furthest reaches of the Greek Isles. They were partners: little black doggie with funny little brown dots over each eye, tall blond American girl striding down the highways and byways of the World.

When they returned to America in 1996, Squiggs was suddenly 10 years old, her face was graying and her hearing was not what it once was. However, her skips remained constant, and her love of raw carrots never once diminished. She had avid admirers there in the State Department who vied for the opportunity to doggie sit when Tracy made short business trips. Flying was no longer an option for after the last trip from Athens, Tracy had promised her that she wouldn't be asked to fly again.

Squiggs had lived her whole life on the "morning side of the mountain" and we refused to believe that her twilight was but a heartbeat away. Her first surgery was in late '96 and the second in '97– tumors. She never missed a skip– until last week when she went in for her 3 month set of X-rays– cancer through and through.

There's a river of tears flowing today, from this Rio Grande Valley to Sterling, Virginia, - - **SQUIGGS GRIGGS**– Lifetime Partner - 1987 to May 2, 1998.

Rocky

When they moved into the new house, a large dog appeared from under the deck to greet them. He was a large dusky Malamute. He approached the new homeowners with slight hesitation, but appeared to be friendly, curious and well mannered. He was in premier condition and his collar had a tag embossed into it saying "If this dog is found– etc." with a Houston telephone number.

The number was promptly called and the lady on the other end of the line questioned "Is the dog a Malamute? Does it have TWO blue eyes? Is it a male?" Then she finally blurted out "You must think I am crazy, but I can't believe it is my dog– MY dog was stolen 3 ½ years ago from our backyard in Houston! We advertised for him for almost a year."

The weekend arrived and with it, driving a pickup with a large dog crate in back, was our lady. She said feared that her two-year-old Malamute (who was now 5 ½) would not recognize her and she prepared herself for the worst.

She quietly said "Hi Rocky." while he warily circled her, sniffing her shoes, then pant legs–- and as suddenly as it all began, he sat down, staring up into her face and cried piteously like a child. He raised himself to his back legs and put his huge paws on her shoulders and licked her face with a joy that made the grown men wipe the tears away. Then she got to her knees to hug him and he fell to the ground on his back– his final gift the "you are still my master" gesture.   He went home to Houston that day, and only Rocky will ever know the story of those three and one half years– and he ain't a tellin'..

Funny, it's always the happy stories that make me cry.

For Pity's Sake

She made headlines and a front-page picture in the Monitor, but it certainly wasn't her finest moment. Perhaps she was a beautiful horse in her prime, and we know for a fact, that she was a decent horse, a horse with a kind eye and a gentle way - she respected her humans and trusted them.

The morning that I found her, there on that gravel road, 'way on the other side of the town, she was dying. My anonymous friend reported her to me (the way she always gives me her injured or abused horse report - by my answering machine) she *told* me that the mare was dying. I found it hard to believe that a horse was dying and no one was caring. But, none the less, Sandy and I took an early morning drive past #107 and 2 1/2 miles north on a dusty, gravel road, sure enough, there, next to the Church, against the road, stood the mare. As we watched her, she raised and lowered her injured leg dozens of times, her eyes were sunken and she listlessly pulled at the blade or two of sparse grass.

I talked to two of the neighbors who told me she "looked better" than she had when she had arrived two months prior to our seeing her. I could not envision *that* sight, and inquired as to the owner of the horse. He was a good, kind man and he did the very best he could, they said. So, I left my card, and asked them to relay to the owner of the mare that I would help him in any way that I could. Before I was a mile down the road, he called me. He was concerned about the horse, but he told me he was a simple man, a poor man who could not afford a veterinary. I asked him if he could confine the mare - to keep her from having to walk a pasture, but he had no facilities. I told him I would take her and try to help her: to confine her and feed and medicate her, and he was readily agreeable.

Calling my neighbors and good friends, Billy and Ginger, I asked for their help to gather the horse. Going back home, I led them in their pickup, pulling their stock trailer, back up the dusty, gravel road. True to his word, the owner had his sister waiting and she opened the gate for us to lead the mare down to the trailer. The mare *wanted* to help us and get right up into the trailer, but she was too weak, so, one by one, Billy lifted and placed her feet in - with me handing out grain pellets and urging her forward. Ginger cried, as she moved ropes and held firm on the halter, during most of the process, and I will admit to a certain lump in my throat as well.

Driving behind the trailer, I was amazed at how courageous the mare was - she gamely stood firm, looking from side to side as they slowly drove back to my place. We got her unloaded and placed in an interior stall, the floor soft with hay, a manger of grain and a pail of cool water. I gave her penicillin shots, a cursory cleaning of the leg wound and several hugs and kind words. She needed food, and she needed rest and a little love couldn't hurt. I ventured out to the barn as night fell, and she was lying down, quietly sleeping.

Morning, 6 am, she was up, the leg swelling down, and I was giddy with enthusiasm. Perhaps, just perhaps we're going to save her. More grain more water and a new clean stall with the morning's warm sun peeking over the wall.

My own horse, Annie (wicked, wicked Annie, the witch of the west) was uncharacteristically quiet with her new stall mate. She watched from across the aisle, and as she walked out to pasture, she stood, head reaching out to touch the injured horse. She was alert to every move and every visit I made.

When Dr. Heflin came to see if we could make the mare well again, he told us straight out. No hope, no way. Putting her to death could only stop the suffering. Even if the disease could be checked, months of stripping bone and flesh, even then, there would have to be skin grafts. Not that she wasn't worth it, but was it worth it to her? The quality of her life had already been hell, but from there to. . what?

So, the next morning, after I had fed her a grand meal and wept into her scrawny neck, I left, not to return until it was all over. They came and with the kindness she deserved and the gentleness she required, they put her to rest. They later told me that my Annie, standing across the fence, ears stretched forward, nostrils flaring, cried out several shrill cries and raced to the far corner of the pasture as the mare went down. A call of fear? A call of friendship? Or, just like the rest of us, a call of mourning.

Bess Brown

Perhaps there are stories that shouldn't be told, but when the air begins to cool, my mind goes back to Rapid City, South Dakota, and Bess Brown, and I re-live the day that she came to our place in Rapid Valley.

Bess belonged to our friend Jody Johnson and was somewhat a local celebrity, as she had spent much of her young life away in Texas being trained. She was a pleasure horse <u>and</u> a confirmation horse, and when she finally came home that year, she had been Grand Champion Mare at the Denver Stock Show.

It was shortly thereafter that Jody called and said that she was feeling badly for Bess. That Bess had spent her whole life in stalls and paddocks, and she would like to have a safe pasture for her to spend a few months, before going back on the horse show circuit. Well, Norm and I were as giddy as kids when she decided to bring her to our place. We indeed had a safe pasture with a spring fed creek running through the meadow, and two hay fields, freshly cut, that beckoned to the horses to graze. Our own two saddle horses were pasture wise, and not aggressive with other horses, so we welcomed Bess Brown to our place early of a Friday morning.

Friday afternoon, when Norm called me from the farm, his voice quavered with emotion– "Bess Brown has broken her leg!" For a horse to break a leg is almost unheard of– especially a pasture horse, but when

I raced for home, sure enough, Bess stood quietly, rear leg dangling. The veterinarian and I arrived almost simultaneously, and what we saw, I hope to never see again, the great mare stood on the other side of the creek, head down, eyes glassy. I ran to the house to call Jody, while the doctor administered a sedative and painkiller. With Bess now on the ground, we had the problem of getting her into the shed– Jaynell, our friend from the farm next door, gingerly lifted her with the front-end loader and backed across the creek and up to the barn. The vet told us he could set the leg, but Jody, Jaynell and I sat on the ground next to Bess, crying and laying our faces against her silken neck.

Once the leg was set, we gingerly lifted her to her feet with the tractor and, with an improvised pulley set-up, we rigged a contraption that we could lower her in the evening and raise her back up during the day.

We, of course, didn't count on the enormous weight of Bess, who must have weighed close to 1200 pounds. No matter how gentle the straps that encompassed her body, they chaffed and ulcerated her skin, and, as the days wore on we felt like we were the perpetrators of a nightmare. As evening would fall, we'd lower her into a bed of straw, and throughout the nights, we would hear her groans and labored breathing.

Jody made the decision, herself; it was time to end the suffering. When the Vet came, it was to inject Bess Brown with, first, a sedative and as we were lowering her that one last time; the injection changed to the fatal one. She sighed a sigh, perhaps of relief, perhaps of joy, that the suffering was over, and she, in fact, this time was going to a safe pasture with many creeks and green fields

We never spoke of Bess after that, perhaps we were ashamed of our inhumanity, or perhaps we just couldn't speak of her courage, as she endured one humiliation after another. Her very kindness in the midst of our ignorance made it hard to forget, and while we never spoke of it again, I would imagine that in the recesses our minds we would always hold a memory of Bess Brown.

Bird Watch

I could see him after he landed in the trees— mainly just the size of him and the breadth of him. He had soared over us there in the yard, and we called out, not necessarily to him, but to ourselves, excited, I guess. Excited, yes, we were excited to see him soar over us— and to land, but a football field away. We dashed to the house for the binoculars, and with elbows propped up on the back fence, we took turns trying to figure out just what he was— back there in his entire splendor.

Tracy had the "bird book" and I the binoculars, and we traded items back and forth, while our giant bird preened there at the tree line in the early morning's light. We originally thought him to be a hawk, but in our eager pawing through the book, to determine just what kind of hawk; we glimpsed the picture of the Golden Eagle, and wondered if, in fact, that was what he was.

We didn't want to troop down there to stare unabashedly from beneath the tree, knowing it would send him soaring, once again, through the skies above us. So with eyes straining, and elbows grinding into the wooden fence, we watched. It amazes me now, to think that we stood there for so long. His back was a mottled gold and brown, and, while the top of his head was flat, it was large and rather defined and he had a hooked beak. He carefully took each feather and cleaned it with demeanor so majestic you would have thought he was touching silk. His wingspan appeared to be about 5 foot, so feather cleaning had to be a tiresome business.

We stood there, with necks craning and eyes straining, another bird entered the scene– scarcely 100 feet from the original bird. This bird we recognized as an Osprey– a large fish eating bird that lives in our general vicinity. He is easily recognizable, as his chest is white, as is his head, with brown wings, back, and little top hat.

It appeared to us, there in the peanut gallery that the two birds simply stared across the treetops at each other. Neither bird moved - no apparent sounds coming back to us - a stare down in the pastures of Griggs. The preening stopped momentarily, and then both birds seemed to get caught up in the morning's cleaning and they stayed side by side for what seemed like a long time.

Then the Osprey unfolded his wings and soared up and over us to places unknown. The giant golden hawk/eagle stayed put, and Tracy asked me what I thought had transpired between them. I told her I thought that they had simply looked at each other and thought to themselves "Deeelicious". The Osprey checking it out further decided to have a fish dinner and left before the stranger decided to have a bird dinner.

Life in the Valley– it doesn't get much better than this.

They're Baaaack!!

Actually, it wasn't much of a clue, but to me it spoke volumes, "They're baaaaack!"

My friend, Ginger, had left this message on my answering machine a week or so ago, and as soon as I heard it, I became a whirlwind of activity. Now, to some one less "in the know" out there in the country, it could have meant that the ghosts were hovering or that the Indian Burial Ground had been discovered beneath our houses, but to me it simply indicated that the Purple Martin scouts were circling.

Now, never let it be said that I could be stampeded into something as homey as being a bird enthusiast, but after my success story last year with my Purple Martins (bought a great looking Martin house in Fredericksburg, 'cause I thought it was pretty) I am feeling pretty darn birdy. There's a lot to this bird stuff, and after arming myself with a book appropriately entitled "Bird Watching For Dummies" - Purple Martin section - I took to the back yard with a perfect watching position.

The magnificent Purple Martin nests, if humanly -(or should I say "birdly" possible?) In the exact same house that she nested last year and the year before. When the baby Martins fly away, they, too, return to the same home (however, at this point, I believe that they are promptly kicked out on their wing to find their own dwelling). Now, should these babies find a new home, within close proximity with Mom and Dad - hey, perfect.

Since last year was my virgin flight into *Purple Martin World*, I probably got some of the baby overrun from my friends and neighbors, the Simpsons. Business was booming last year, and my six-room condo birdhouse was filled to the brim with moms, dads and ultimately babies. We suffered a few tragedies, a baby fell into the pool and died, a baby fell to the ground or, quite possibly, into Slick's watering mouth, and was no longer a contender and I rescued one adventurer from the pool, dried him off and he flew off into the wild blue, sun glistening off of his iridescent wings.

But, now to the "they're baaak" remark - Purple Martins send scouts ahead to make certain that their old home hasn't been rented out, or ruined by an influx of Sparrows! To make certain that this doesn't happen (I'm told) we lower our houses, clean them out at the end of the season (October) and await the arrival of the scout at the beginning of the next season.... Yesterday was that day.

With super human strength, a hammer, a screw driver, wedges and a great deal of huffing and puffing, I raised my last years house (what a beauty it is - looks like a castle with little flags on the individual roofs) to it's grand heights and looked to the skies. Of course, a new bird watcher such as myself could not allow babies to return to my yard and be interlopers, homeless, and/or unwanted, so, of course, the next time in Fredericksburg we bought two new Purple Martin houses.

So now, the dragging of the poles, and the placing of the wedges and the fastening together of the sides and the, once again, raising the houses to all new and wondrous heights. The new castle house has a blue set of roofs and the new "strange" set of condos is made up of eight white plastic, gourd looking houses, that swing precariously in the evening breeze. I wish I could tell you that it was a smooth installation, one without the pole sliding down on the fleshy side of my finger, making me scream out very unbirdly sounds, or the pole sliding down to conk me on the head with a gourd, but that, actually would take some of the adventure out of it.

But the houses are now up - I await my guests with enthusiasm. I must be vigilant, I must keep other birds at bay, I must be prepared to battle the Starlings and the Sparrows. My evenings will be spent with eyes scanning the skies. .... I must get a life.

The Hawk & I

The Hawk and I have reached an agreement here of late. He may live in my trees, without me running and waving my arms to alarm him into leaving, and he will let me walk close enough to him to see the full breadth of him and look into his clear eyes.

He and I have been yard mates for several years now, but until last year, we really hadn't "come to terms". He's brave, my Hawk, and I may walk beneath him if I play like I don't see him, and he has been known to fearlessly swoop down but yards from me to snatch up a ground squirrel and soar into the skies. I know that he preys on the small rabbits and rats that live in the fields around me, and I don't begrudge him his feasting. He's neat, my Hawk, and he dives without a sound, hitting, killing and sweeping off to eat in some close by place.

Seems but a few weeks ago, that I stood on my usual observation point on the diving board, looking skyward. With hands shielding my eyes, I saw, what appeared to be dozens of scraps of black confetti sifting through the sky. Then, refocusing, I could see hawks, hundreds of hawks— soaring over me. Two of them, then three of them circled over the irrigation ditch, lower and lower, giant wings spreading gracefully out, tips turning out into the wind.

On that very day, MY Hawk returned to the trees around the house, and I could see him in the live oak tree, chocolate brown feathers now blending into the early leaves. I suppose that the hawks go up north for the summer and return to us for the warm winters here in the Valley. While I had not observed their migration before, I now constantly scan the skies for them. It appears that they fly higher than the other birds, and you don't even see them unless one or two have "jobs" on the surface somewhere close.

The other day around noon, the guineas were raising all sorts of Cain behind the fence of my yard, and when I stood on tiptoes to peer over the fence, to ask them to settle down, there sat my Hawk, eating the remainder of my favorite Bantam Hen. He casually looked up at me, and continued his dining. (In his mind, this apparently fell into the "I don't bother you, you don't bother me" category that we had already established.) The guineas continued their grousing and I dashed out the garage door to see if there was any hope at all. My Hawk pretty much ignored me at first (he thought she was part of our deal, I guess) then I did the arm waving and yelling thing and he leisurely flew into the nearby oak tree.

I put the Banty's body (the remains of the day) over beside the driveway, and as I was walking away, my Hawk returned to polish off his lunch. Think I am going to have to revise my contract with him...

Wings Of The Wind

My hawk rides on the wings of the wind this morning, and I look into the sky and smile as he rocks gracefully, his own wings stretching out— higher and lower and through the air.

He has been my companion for so long now, I miss seeing him circling above the pasture, when he is hunting away from "our" pasture. He is ever faithful to me here though, and while he, perhaps, catches a rat or two and maybe, just maybe, a rabbit, I know that he covets my little band of chickens that live around the barn. He has been driven to catching domestic animals now that the Simpson property is pristine, with mowed fields and children playing on the gym equipment. When the farm animals lived in the pastures next door, the fields were alive with small, Hawk-yummy, animals, and he left my chickens living in peace.

He stalked my favorite chicken, "Sunshine" for several weeks. She was hatched here, and went on to be such a good mom to baby chicks (and one crazy time— two guinea eggs hatched and she thought— and THEY thought— she was their mom). She had escaped him many times; one time she showed up with no tail feathers and stayed inside the hay stall for several weeks. Sure enough, when she ventured out, she was plucked naked from chest to head, but she came back. By now, I was worried enough to put baffles across the ends of the barn, to detour him as he swept through the walkway to snatch up some tasty morsel.

As I would walk to the barn early of a morning, I would look for "Sunshine"– calling out for her to come and get morning chow. She normally obliged, but early one morning, just after the sun had come up, I called, and lo and behold, no "Sunshine". I walked the stalls and I circled the barn (thinking, all the time, to myself, that she was, in fact, too heavy for my Hawk to kill, too big and too agile).

In my peripheral vision, behind the wooden fence that circles my back yard, I see a strange sight: my Hawk sitting complacently. With furrowed brow and heavy heart, I walked to the fence, sitting but a few feet from me he sat– he sat atop "Sunshine" who, of course, was dead. He had his claws sunk into her golden feathers– and didn't move an eyelash as I walked up to him. He found himself in a position that many of us have found ourselves.

He had made her his project and he worked for weeks to achieve his goal. Alas, however, now that he had her– now what? Ahora Que? She was too heavy to carry off into the air, and he couldn't leave her because something else might take her. So there he sat. His wishes fulfilled, but I wonder if he wasn't thinking, as I have thought many times, mid-project, what in the World do I do now. When things get too big for me these days, I think of my Hawk, sitting there atop "Sunshine"– and wonder if that tremendous effort is, in fact, worth the outcome?

For The Birds

When I saw the invitation "State of the Art Bird Museum in Saltillo" I immediately thought that we had to go– but, I didn't relish the thought of the trip– leaving early– 6:30 am and then the drive - phew. Of course, then I wondered who all was going, what to wear, how critical the information we were to give and how critical the information we were to receive. Worry, worry.

Getting ideas to integrate into Quinta Mazatlan, our very own, (we say prayerfully) World Birding Center was enough incentive to get me out to the bus on time. Then, guess what? It was old home week– most of the folks were old friends; tour guide Wayne Showers and Reba were enthusiastically greeting the arrivals and giving promises of breakfast on the road. A bus full of bird enthusiasts chattering bird info– plus the usual, so– what's happening in your life and what's new in the City, pretty much tided us over 'til we reached Ramos Arizpe, Coah.

Then, it was "ShowTime"– our fearless leader, shared with us a story about the owner/chef of the French Restaurant, Jean Luis. And some story it was! The story was surpassed only by the food, and we ate and visited and spoke about "Aves de Saltillo", the Bird Museum in Saltillo– Wayne had been there and promised that we would love it. We weren't all that certain– stuffed birds? (Had we but known the extent of the "stuffed bird" premise, we would have been begging for them to speed up and get us there immediately).

After checking in at the hotel, we readied ourselves for the museum— still doubtful. Founder and owner of the museum, Aldegundo Garza de Leon and his wife, Bessie Nelson de Garza greeted us and introduced us to our guides– children docents who attend a bilingual school similar to the Oratory Academy in Pharr. Our forty person group was quickly divided up between guides (each of us thought that OUR guide was the best guide there!)and away we went. When they told us we would possibly be there for 2 to 3 hours, I went faint with fear– 2 to 3 hours looking at stuffed birds? You've got to be kidding!

Well, folks, 2 and1/2 hours later, neck stiff from rubber necking, I was sick to see the tour end. 2000 birds– tastefully displayed, sound effects, natural habitat settings, 1000 of the species found in Mexico and the "run off" effect of conservation and preservation continuing in Mexico.

As we stood outside of the museum, saying our "Good Byes" we were stunned as a fledgling bird plummeted into our midst from one of the towering trees above us. A worried mommy Dove hovered overhead until we rescued it and placed it back into the crook of the tree. We kidded Sr.Garza de Leon that it was a set up, and he, good-naturedly, admitted that he had conspired with the mom Dove.

Saltillo is a particular favorite of mine, clean, friendly with beautiful mountain scenery, and now, a fabulous bird museum? What more could you require? Our museum host Sr. Garza de Leon and his wife joined us for a late dinner at La Canasta– again wonderful food, great company and much snatching food from other tables! We were out of control (again) and loved it! Kay Jantzen and sister, Susie Robertson were great sports as our table shared "their" table– I thought that Chuck Snyder might launch a counter attack along with the Clarks, but, surprisingly, they behaved better than we did. David Whitlock was, actually, the chief troublemaker, but who's to throw stones?

It was an inspirational trip with all of the right ingredients– convivial travelers, great food, and sights to stagger the imagination. I congratulate

The Valley Land Fund for arranging this trip and hope that I didn't misbehave enough to be excluded from the next trip!

The Nutria

I saw them for the first time many, many years ago. My big dog, Slick, and I walked along the canal and irrigation ditches that parallel Bicentennial Blvd. It was a two-mile stint, and we walked it every day at 5 PM. Actually, I walked and Slicked tugged ahead thinking he was 'on to something' at every crossroad and clump of bushes.

Perhaps we had gone a bit later that day, because the shadows were long as we approached the ditch. Slick had his nose into every, what HE hope to be, burrow and I was just sort of on idle when I spied some movement from within the waterway. It was just a quick movement, no more. I moved over closer to the edge and peered down into the very eyes of the biggest rat I ever saw in my life. I gave an "oooff" sound and scrambled back— well, it scared him twice as much because I saw him go hustling back down into the water and across into what could have been Slick's dream "burrow".

In a frantic call to our then Mayor, Mayor Brand (wish he could have seen MY end of *that* conversation) I explained step by step my encounter with the "probably 10 pound rat". My arms were waving, my hands were measuring and my voice was rising. He just chuckled and said, "That was no rat, sweetheart, that was nutria." Nutria? Yep, a nutria. He said the nutria had been brought into the Valley some 50 or 60 years ago to keep the waterways clean from weeds and other foliage that would hinder the progress of floodwater leaving the City.

The explanation made perfect sense to me and on our walks thereafter; I walked closely to the edge and continued to make an occasional sighting. I loved the big furry creatures after that, felt that they had their job to do and they were doing it. After all, they were *invited* here and could be considered part of our community. Well, let's not go just plain nuts here, but I felt that if they stayed in their own community I would be happy for them.

Several years later I heard some gentlemen talking about taking their teenage sons down to the ditches to shoot the nutria. I was outraged. Not only had I thought at that point that the nutria were MY secret, but to kill something living that had a useful purpose was beyond my imagination. I did make this known to them and they gave me the eye-roll that only a man talking to an animal nut can make— the "hoooo boy" look.

Now, we have the walking and jogging trails some distance from the ditch on Bicentennial and I see that the County Irrigation District is putting the irrigation canal under ground. There are workers and trucks in the ditch area, and I wonder about the nutria? Do they continue to do their jobs into the night?

Are they fleeing from the noises and the commotion? Are they, like the coyotes driven from the hustle and bustle of a City on the move?

Where have the nutria gone?

Bob

God sent Bob to me. I believe that as certainly as I believe that Bob is here next to my desk, snoring loudly and shedding profusely. It's a long story, my love affair with this giant dog. When my big dog, Slick, was 12, he was still looking very "slick-like"– full of energy, running, barking– all of the stuff that a big dog is suppose to do. The hair on his tail was gone, but hey– that's a long way from his heart, I thought. Hmm, I guess I thought wrong as his heart was weakened and his other organs were failing as well. I refused to believe and as he and I played that last night, the night he died, he appeared to me to be healthy.... But then again, this is a story about Bob.

I had accidentally seen Bob at a Kennel in Harlingen a year before Slick had died. Wow– I admired him to the Kennel owner, Kathy Hines. She said that he belonged to a gentleman from Marble Falls, who had left him for "a spell" as he (the owner) ridded himself of cancer. The cancer eventually won, and Bobby was left at the Kennel– a four year old American Bulldog who had never lived in a house. A magnificent kennel dog one might say and the skinless patches on his elbows attested to the fact that he lived on concrete. When Kathy called me several months after I had first seen Bob, I was surprised that she said she was going to give Bobby to me! Huh?!

Well now, I made it perfectly clear that I had Slick and Slick was fine and—

She didn't take it for the gospel and came up and starred at Slick. Hmmm, he is an old doggie she said— and he will die in a few months! I reeled back in horror, but when her prediction came true within the next six months, I called her "Kathy? I am coming down for Bobby."

Bear in mind that Bobby and I had never "officially" met— I had seen him, admired him there in his kennel, but insofar as a personal eyeball to eyeball meeting— nope. He came with me, obligingly, rope around his neck and big time kennel smell around the rest of him, and sat quietly in the back of the 4-Runner. When I stopped to get him a collar, I found that his neck was 26 inches— and for a brief moment I recalled my waist once being 26 inches.

He came into the house and did inspecting— I'm certain that trails of Slick covered the furniture and the carpets— and he sniffed and he snuffed and when I pushed him out the doggy door— he became a house dog. After I lifted him into the bathtub and gave him a long, long bath, he became MY house dog.

At first he slept by the garage door— I suppose he wanted to go back to familiar surroundings. Then he slept in the kitchen at night, and then, as a mutual affection came to us, he slept by the sofa— by me.

There in that familiar position, on my side, pillow under my head, watching something TV— a position that Slick and I shared every night, with him curled in the curve of my knees— something amazing happened. Bob lay his great head at my feet on the couch, I moved my legs aside and he stepped up to the sofa, did the best he could in fitting into the curve of my legs. God sent Bob to me— and he let me know it that night when we "spooned" there on the couch. I cried, of course, and told God that I *knew*—

I have Bob now for seven going on eight years. He is deaf, but has a nose that can tell when I open the door. His heart is failing, but he still plays with his ball. My 106 pound Bob— a cast away who found himself claimed by another cast away. My boy, Bob. Thank you, God. Thank you.

Epilogue

As my "affair" with this book ends, all is well here at the farm. Cowboy, the erasable yellow-headed parrot who flew into my back yard 17 years ago, is sitting with the bell on her head. Bob is snoring like a pack-mule on the floor here next to me. Annie, wicked, wicked Annie my grey mare is standing under the mesquite tree. Her goat, Dinah, is never far away from "her" horse and they enjoy a cool breeze.

The Guineas are in the front yard, nipping off the tender grass shoots, and the rooster and the two hens have dug in under the Yucca.

The Purple Martins circle high in the morning sky, and for the thousandth time I wonder where they go when they are not here.

The green parrots circle, but have not returned to the tree in the back yard, soon they will come back and raise another family in the palm tree next to the pool

I cautiously look into Grandma's bedroom to see if the Pigmy Owls have returned to the window ledge outside; they quietly sit on the wrought iron railing.

All is well.

Divorced in 1972, one child, Tracy Griggs, who graduated from McHi in 1982 and from SMU in 1986. She has worked in Amman, Jordan and Athens, Greece as Admin-Officer in our United States Embassies. Recently moved back to the United States and works in Washington, DC, for the State Department. She played basketball for McHi – was All-Valley, All-District, All-State and Captain of her team and graduated 24th out of her graduating class of 800+-. (That just gave me the opportunity to brag a bit! – Thanks!)